ZEELAND COSTUMES

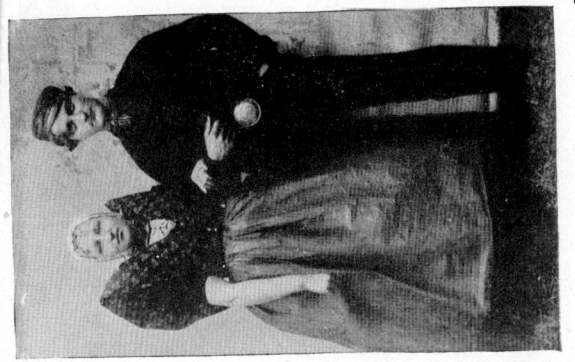

OUR EUROPEAN NEIGHBOURS

French Life
   German Life
      Russian Life
         Dutch Life
            Swiss Life
               Spanish Life
Italian Life
   Danish Life
      Austro-Hungarian Life
         Turkish Life
            Belgian Life
               Swedish Life

OUR EUROPEAN
NEIGHBOURS

EDITED BY
WILLIAM HARBUTT DAWSON

DUTCH LIFE IN TOWN AND
COUNTRY

THE DELFT GATE AT ROTTERDAM

DUTCH LIFE IN TOWN AND COUNTRY

By P. M. HOUGH, B.A.

ILLUSTRATED

G. P. PUTNAM'S SONS
NEW YORK AND LONDON
The Knickerbocker Press
1911

COPYRIGHT, 1901
BY
G. P. PUTNAM'S SONS

Set up, electrotyped, and printed November, 1901
Reprinted, January, 1902 ; August, 1902 ; March 1903
September, 1903 ; December, 1904 ; June, 1905 ; April, 1906
April, 1909 ; January, 1911

DJ
71
H83

The Knickerbocker Press, New York

CONTENTS

CHAPTER I
NATIONAL CHARACTERISTICS 1

CHAPTER II
COURT AND SOCIETY 11

CHAPTER III
THE PROFESSIONAL CLASSES 21

CHAPTER IV
THE POSITION OF WOMEN 37

CHAPTER V
THE WORKMAN OF THE TOWNS 50

CHAPTER VI
THE CANALS AND THEIR POPULATION . . 63

CHAPTER VII
A DUTCH VILLAGE 76

CHAPTER VIII
THE PEASANT AT HOME 83

CHAPTER IX
RURAL CUSTOMS 99

CHAPTER X
KERMIS AND ST. NICHOLAS 114

Contents

CHAPTER XI
NATIONAL AMUSEMENTS 132

CHAPTER XII
MUSIC AND THE THEATRE 145

CHAPTER XIII
SCHOOLS AND SCHOOL LIFE 154

CHAPTER XIV
THE UNIVERSITIES 167

CHAPTER XV
ART AND LETTERS 179

CHAPTER XVI
THE DUTCH AS READERS 193

CHAPTER XVII
POLITICAL LIFE AND THOUGHT 207

CHAPTER XVIII
THE ADMINISTRATION OF JUSTICE 221

CHAPTER XIX
RELIGIOUS LIFE AND THOUGHT 235

CHAPTER XX
THE ARMY AND NAVY 247

CHAPTER XXI
HOLLAND OVER SEA 264

INDEX 289

ILLUSTRATIONS

	PAGE
THE DELFT GATE AT ROTTERDAM *Frontispiece*	
TYPES OF ZEELAND WOMEN	6
ZEELAND COSTUMES	38
DUTCH FISHER-GIRLS	46
AN OVERYSSEL FARMHOUSE	58
A SEA-GOING CANAL	66
A VILLAGE IN DYKE-LAND	76
ZEELAND WOMEN, THE DARK TYPES	84
INTERIOR OF FARMHOUSE, SHOWING OPEN FIRE ON THE FLOOR	88
INTERIOR OF FARMHOUSE, SHOWING DOOR BETWEEN STABLE AND LIVING-ROOM	96
PALM PASCHEN—BEGGING FOR EGGS	100
KERMIS—"HOSSEN-HOSSEN-HI-HA" After the picture by Van Geldrop.	110
ZEELAND COSTUMES	124
A CANAL IN DORDRECHT	144
PARLIAMENT HOUSE AT THE HAGUE. VIEW FROM THE GREAT LAKE	210
INTERIOR OF THE CHURCH AT DELFTSHAVEN WHERE THE PILGRIM FATHERS WORSHIPPED BEFORE LEAVING FOR NEW ENGLAND	238

DUTCH LIFE IN TOWN AND COUNTRY

CHAPTER I

NATIONAL CHARACTERISTICS

THERE is in human affairs a reason for everything we see, although not always reason in everything. It is the part of the historian to seek in the archives of a nation the reasons for the facts of common experience and observation; it is the part of the philosopher to moralise upon antecedent causes and present results. Neither of these positions is taken up by the author of this little book. He merely, as a rule, gives the picture of Dutch life now to be seen in the Netherlands, and in all things tries to be scrupulously fair to a people renowned for their kindness and courtesy to the stranger in their midst.

And this strikes one first about Holland—that everything, except the old Parish Churches, the

Town Halls, the dykes, and the trees, is in miniature. The cities are not populous; the houses are not large; the canals are not wide; and one can go from the most northern point in the country to the most southern, or from the extreme east to the extreme west, in a single day, and, if it be a summer's day, in *daylight*, while from the top of the tower of the Cathedral at Utrecht one can look over a large part of the land.

As it is with the natural so it is with the political horizon. This latter embraces for the average Dutchman the people of a country whose interests seem to him bound up for the most part in the twelve thousand square miles of lowland pressed into a corner of Europe; for, extensive as the Dutch colonies are, they are not "taken in" by the average Dutchman as are the colonies of some other nations. There are one or two towns, such as The Hague and Arnhem, where an Indo-Dutch society may be found, consisting of retired colonial civil servants, who very often have married Indian women, and have either returned home to live on well-earned pensions or who prefer to spend the money gained in India in the country which gave them birth. But Holland has not yet begun to develop as far as she might the great resources of Netherlands India, and therefore no very great amount of interest is taken in the colonial possessions outside merely home, official, or Indo-Dutch society.

With regard to the affairs of his country generally, the state of mind of the average Dutchman has been well described as that of a man well on in years, who has amassed a fair fortune, and now takes things easily, and loves to talk over the somewhat wild doings of his youth. Nothing is more common than to hear the remarks from both old and young, "We *have* been great," "We have *had* our time," "Every nation reaches a climax"; and certainly Holland has been very great in statesmen, patriots, theologians, artists, explorers, colonisers, soldiers, sailors, and martyrs. The names of William the Silent, Barneveldt, Arminius, Rembrandt, Rubens, Hobbema, Grotius, De Ruyter, Erasmus, Ruysdaël, Daendels, Van Speijk and Van Tromp afford proof of the pertinacity, courage, and devotion of Netherlands' sons in the great movements which have sprung from her soil.

To have successfully resisted the might of a Philip of Spain and the strategy and cruelties of an Alva is alone a title-deed to imperishable fame and honour. Dutch men and women fought and died at the dykes, and suffered awful agonies on the rack and at the stake. "They sang songs of triumph," so the record runs, "while the grave-diggers were shovelling earth over their living faces." It is not, therefore, to be wondered at that a legacy of true and deep feeling has been bequeathed to their descendants, and the very suspicion of injustice or infringement of what they consider liberty sets the Dutchman's heart aflame with patriotic devotion or private resentment. Phlegmatic, even comal, and most difficult to move in most things, yet any "interference" wakes up the dormant spirit which that Prince of Orange so forcibly expressed when he said, in response to a prudent soldier's fear of consequences if resistance were persisted in, "We can at least die in the last ditch."

Until one understands this tenacity in the Dutch character one cannot reconcile the old-world methods seen all over the country with the advanced ideas expressed in conversation, books, and newspapers. The Dutchman hates to be interfered with, and resents the advice of candid friends, and cannot stand any "chaff." He has his kind of humour, which is slow in expression and material in conception, but he does not understand "banter." He is liberal in theories, but intensely conservative in practice. He will *agree* with a new theory, but often *do* as his grandfather did, and so in Holland there may be seen very primitive methods side by side with *fin de siècle* thought. In a *salon* in any principal town there will be thought the most advanced, and manner of life the most luxurious, but a stone's throw off, in a cottage or in a farmhouse just outside the town, may be witnessed the life of the seventeenth century. Some of the reasons for this may be gathered from the following pages as they describe the social life and usages of the people.

National Characteristics

In the seven provinces which comprise the Netherlands there are considerable differences in scenery, race, dialect, pronunciation, and religion, and therefore in the features and character of the people. United provinces in the course of time effect a certain homogeneity of purpose and interest, yet there are certain fundamental differences in character. The Frisian differs from the Zeelander: one is fair and the other dark, and both differ from the Hollander. And not only do the provincials differ in character, dialect, and pronunciation from one another, but also the inhabitants of some cities differ in these respects from those of other cities. An educated Dutchman can tell at once if a man comes from Amsterdam, Rotterdam, or The Hague. The "cockney" of these places differs, and of such pronunciations "Hague Dutch" is considered the worst, although—true to the analogy of London—the best Dutch is heard in The Hague. This difference in "civic" pronunciation is certainly very remarkable when one remembers that The Hague and Rotterdam are only sixteen miles apart, and The Hague and Amsterdam only forty miles. Arnhem and The Hague are the two most cosmopolitan cities in the kingdom, and one meets in their streets all sorts and conditions of the Netherlander.

All other towns are provincial in character and akin to the county-town type. Even Amsterdam, the capital of the country, is only a commercial capital. The Court is there only for a few days in each year; Parliament does not meet there ; the public offices are not situated there ; and diplomatic representatives are not accredited to the Court at Amsterdam but to the Court at The Hague ; and so Amsterdam is "the city," and no more and no less. This Venice of the North looks coldly on the pleasure seeking and loving Hague, and jealously on the thriving and rapidly increasing port of Rotterdam, and its merchant princes build their villas in the neighbouring and pleasant woods of Bussum and Hilversum, and near the brilliantly-coloured bulb-gardens of Haarlem, living in these suburban places during the summer months, while in winter they return to the fine old houses in the Heerengracht and the many other *grachten* through which the waters of the canals move slowly to the river. But to The Hague the city magnates seldom come, and the young men consider their contemporaries of the Court capital wanting in energy and initiative, and very proud, and so there is little communication between the two towns—between the City and Belgravia. One knows, as one walks in the streets of Amsterdam, The Hague, Rotterdam, or Utrecht, that each place is a microcosm devoted to its own particular and narrow interests, and in these respects they are survivals of the Italian cities of the Middle Ages. There is, indeed, great similarity in the style of buildings, and, with the excep-

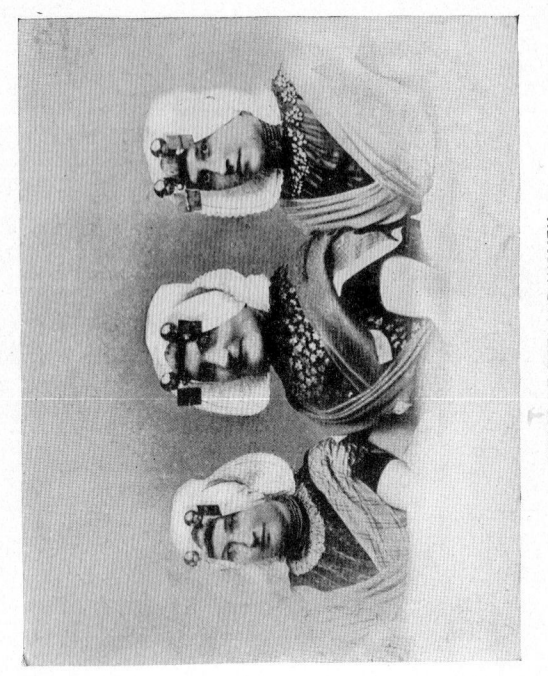

TYPES OF ZEELAND WOMEN

tion of Maestricht, in the south of the country, which is mediæval and Flemish, one always feels that one is in Holland. The neatness of the houses, the straight trees fringing the roads, the canals and their smell, the steam-trams, the sound of the conductor's horn and the bells of the horse-trams, the type of policeman, and above and beyond all the universal cigar—all these things are of a pattern, and that pattern is seen everywhere, and it is not until one has lived in the country for some time that one recognises that there are differences in the mode of life in the larger towns which are more real than apparent, and that this practical isolation is not realised by the stranger.

The country life of the peasant, however, is much more uniform in character, in spite of the many differences in costume and in dialect. The methods of agriculture are all equally old-fashioned, and the peasants equally behind the times in thought. Their thrifty habits and devotion to the soil of their country ensure them a living which is thrown away by the country folk of other lands, who at the first opportunity flock into the towns. But the Dutch peasant *is* a peasant, and does not mix, or want to mix, with the townsman except in the way of business. He brings his garden and farm produce for sale, and as soon as that is effected — generally very much to his own advantage, for he is wonderfully " slim "—he rattles back, drawn by his dogs or little pony, to the farmhouse, and relates how he has come safely back, his stock of produce diminished, but his stock of inventions and subtleties improved and increased by contact with housewives and shopkeepers, who do their best to drive a hard bargain. In dealing with the " boer " the townspeople's ingenuity is taxed to the utmost in endeavouring to get the better of one whose nature is heavy but cunning, and families who have dealt with the same " boer " vendor for years have to be as careful as if they were transacting business with an entire stranger. The " boer's " argument is simplicity itself: " They try to get the better of me, and I try to get the better of them "—and he *does* it!

If, however, there are these differences between city and city and class and class, there is one common characteristic of the Dutchman which, like the mist which envelops meadow and street alike in Holland after a warm day, pertains to the whole race, viz., his deliberation, that slowness of thought, speech, and action which has given rise to such proverbs as " You will see such and such a thing done ' in a Dutch month.' " The Netherlander is most difficult to move, but once roused he is far more difficult to pacify. Many reasons are given for this " phlegm," and most people attribute it to the climate, which is very much abused, especially by Dutch people themselves, because of its sunlessness during the winter months; though as a matter of fact the climate is not so very different from that in the greater part of England. The temperature on an average is a little higher in summer and a little lower in winter than in the eastern part of England ; but certainly there is in the southern part of the country a softness in the air which is enervating, and in such places as Flushing snow is seldom seen, and does not lie long ; but the same thing is seen in Cornwall. Hence this climatic influence is not a sufficient reason in itself to account for the undeniable and general " slowness " of the Dutchman. It is to be found rather in the history of the country, which has taught the Netherlander to attempt to prove by other people's experience the value of new ideas, and only when he has done so will he adopt them. This saps all initiative.

There is a great lack of faith in everything, in secular as well as religious matters ; the Dutchman will risk nothing ; for four cents' outlay he must be quite certain of six cents in return. As long as he is in this mood the country will " mark time," but not advance much. The Dutchman believes so thoroughly in being comfortable, and, given a modest income which he has inherited or gained, he will not only not go a penny beyond it in his expenditure, but often he will live very much below it. He would never think of " living up to " his income ; his idea is to leave his children something very tangible in the shape of gulden. A small income and little or no work is a far more agreeable prospect than a really busy life allied to a large income. All the cautiousness of the Scotchman the Dutchman has, but not the enterprise and industry. With his cosmopolitanism, which he has gained by having to learn and converse in so many languages, in order to transact the large transfer business of such a country as the Netherlands, he has acquired all the various views of life which cosmopolitanism opens to a man's mind. The Dutchman can talk upon politics extremely well, but his interest is largely academic and not personal ; he is as a man who looks on and loves *desipere in loco*.

The Dutchman is therefore a philosopher and a delightful *raconteur*, but at present he is not doing any very great things in the international battle of life, though when great necessity arises there is no man who can do more or do better.

CHAPTER II

COURT AND SOCIETY

SOCIETY life in Holland is, as everywhere else, the gentle art of escaping self-confession of boredom. But society in Holland is far different from society abroad, because The Hague, the official residence of Queen Wilhelmina, is not only not the capital of her kingdom, but is only the third town of the country so far as importance and population go. The Hague is the royal residence and the seat of the Netherlands Government, but although, as a rule, Cabinet Ministers live there, most of the members of the First Chamber of the States-General live elsewhere, and a great many of their colleagues of the Second Chamber follow their example, preferring a couple of hours' railway travelling per day or per week during the time the States sit, to a permanent stay. Hence, so far as political importance goes, society has to do without it to a great extent. Nor is The Hague a centre of science. The universities of Leyden, Utrecht, and Amsterdam are very near, but as the Dutch proverb judiciously says, "Nearly is not half";

there is a vast difference between having the rose and the thing next to it. In consequence the leading scientific men of the Netherlands do not, as a rule, add the charm of their conversation to social intercourse at The Hague.

High life there is represented by members of the nobility and by such high officials in the army, navy, and civil service as mix with that nobility. Of course there are sets just as there are everywhere else, sets as delightful to those who are in them as they are distasteful to outsiders; but talent and money frequently succeed in making serious inroads upon the preserves of noble birth. This is, however, unavoidable, for the Netherlands were a republic for two centuries, and the scions of the ancient houses are not over-numerous. They fought well in the wars of their country against Spain, France, and Great Britain, but fighting well in many cases meant extermination.

On the other hand, two centuries of republican rule are apt to turn any republicans into patricians, particularly so if they are prosperous, self-confident, and well aware of their importance. And a patrician republic necessarily turns into an oligarchy. The prince-merchants of Holland were Holland's statesmen, Holland's absolute rulers; two centuries of heroic struggles, intrepid energy, crowned with success on all sides, may even account for their belief that they were entrusted by the Almighty with a special mission

Court and Society

to bring liberty, equal rights, and prosperity to other nations.

When, after Napoleon's downfall, the Netherlands constituted themselves a kingdom, the depleted ranks of the aristocracy were soon amply filled from these old patrician families. Clause 65 of the Netherlands Constitution says, " The Queen grants nobility. No Dutchman may accept foreign nobility." This is the only occasion upon which the word nobility appears in any code. No Act defines the status, privileges, or rights of this nobility, because there are none. There is, however, a *Hooge Raad van Adel*, consisting of a permanent chairman, a permanent secretary, and four members, whose functions it is to report on matters of nobility, especially heraldic and genealogic, and on applications from Town Councils which wish to use some crest or other. This " High Council of Nobility " acts under the supervision of the Minister of Justice, and its powers are regulated by royal decrees, or writs in council. The titles used are *Jonkheer* (Baronet) and *Jonkvrouw*, Baron and Baroness, *Graaf*, (Earl) and *Gravin*. Marquess and Duke are not used as titles by Dutch noblemen. If any man is ennobled, all his children, sons as well as daughters, share the privilege, so there is no " courtesy title "; officially they are indicated by the father's rank from the moment of their birth, but as long as they are young, it is the custom to address the boys as *Jonker*, the girls as *Freule*.

For the rest, life at The Hague is very much like life everywhere else. In summer there is a general exodus to foreign countries; in winter, dinners, bazaars, balls, theatre, opera, a few official Court functions, which may become more numerous in the near future if the young Queen and Prince Henry are so disposed, are the order of the day. For the present, " Het Loo," that glorious country-seat in the centre of picturesque, hilly, wooded Gelderland, continues to be the favourite residence of the Court, and only during the colder season is the palace in the " Noordeinde," at The Hague, inhabited by the Queen.

Her Majesty, apparently full of youthful mirth and energy, enjoys her life in a wholesome and genuine manner. State business is, of course, dutifully transacted, but as the entire constitutional responsibility rests with the Cabinet Ministers and the High Councils of State, she has no need to feel undue anxiety about her decisions. She is well educated, a strong patriot, and has on the whole a serious turn of mind, which came out in pathetic beauty as she took the oath in the " Nieuwe Kerk " of Amsterdam at her coronation. How far she and her husband will influence and lead society life in Holland remains to be seen. Both are young and their union is younger still. During the late King's life and Queen Emma's subsequent widowhood, society

Court and Society

was for scores of years left to itself, and of course it has settled down into certain grooves. But, on the other hand, the tastes and inclinations of well-bred, well-to-do-people, with an inexhaustible amount of spare time on their hands, and an unlimited appetite for amusement in their minds, are everywhere the same. Of course, Ministerial receptions, political dinners, and the intercourse of Ambassadors and foreign Ministers at The Hague form a special feature of social life there, but here, again, The Hague is just like European capitals generally.

Once every year the Dutch Court and the Dutch capital proper meet. Legally, by the way, it is inaccurate to indicate even Amsterdam as the capital of Holland ; no statute mentions a capital of the kingdom, but by common consent Amsterdam, being the largest and most important town, is always accorded that title, so highly valued by its inhabitants. The Royal Palace in Amsterdam is royal enough, and it is also sufficiently palatial, but it is no Royal Palace in the strict sense of the word. It was built (1649–1655), and for centuries was used, as a Town Hall. As such it is a masterpiece, and one's imagination can easily go back to the times when the powerful and masterful Burgomasters and Sheriffs met in the almost oppressing splendour of its vast hall. It is an ideal meeting-place for stern merchants, enterprising ship-owners, and energetic traders. Every hall, every room, every ornament speaks of trade, trade, and trade again. And there lies some grim irony in the fact that these merchants, whose meeting-place is surmounted by the proud symbol of Atlas carrying the globe, offered that mansion as a residence to their kings, when Holland and Amsterdam could no longer boast of supporting the world by their wealth and their energy.

Here they meet once a year—the stern, ancient city, represented by its sturdy citizens, its fair women, its proud inhabitants, and Holland's youthful Queen, blossoming forth as a symbol of new, fresh life, fresh hope and promise. Here they meet, the sons and daughters of the men and women who never gave way, who saw their immense riches accrue, as their liberties grew, by sheer force of will, by inflexible determination, by dauntless power of purpose; here they meet, the last descendant of the famous House of Orange-Nassau, the queenly bride, whose forefathers were well entitled to let their proud war-cry resound on the battlefields of Europe : *À moi, généreux sang de Nassau !*

When the Queen is in Amsterdam the citizens go out to the "Dam," the Square where the palace stands, offering their homage by cheers and waving of hats, and by singing the war-psalm of the old warriors of William the Silent, *Wilhelmus van Nassouwe.* Then the leaders of Amsterdam, its merchants, scientists, and artists, leave their beautiful homes on Heeren-

Court and Society

and Keizers-gracht, with their wives and daughters wrapped in costly garments, glittering in profusion of diamonds and rubies and pearls, and drive to the huge palace to offer homage to their Queen, just as proud as she, just as patriotic as she, just as faithful and loyal as she.

Three hundred years have done their incessant work in welding the House of Orange and Amsterdam together; ruptures and quarrels have occurred; yet, after every struggle, both found out that they could not well do without each other; and now when the Queen and the city meet, mutual respect, mutual confidence, and reciprocal affection attest the firm bond which unites them.

To the Amsterdam patriciate the yearly visit of the Queen is a social function full of interest. To the Queen it is more than that; she visits not only the patricians, she also visits the people, the poor and the toilers. Of course Amsterdam has its Socialists, and a good many of them, too, and Socialists are not only fiery but also vociferous republicans as a rule, who believe that royalty and a queen are a blot upon modern civilisation. But their sentiments, however well uttered, are not popular. For when " Our Child," as the Queen is still frequently called, drives through the workmen's quarter of Amsterdam, the " Jordaan " (a corruption of the French *jardin*), the bunting is plentiful, the cheering and singing are more so, and the general enthusiasm surpasses both. The "man in the street," that remarkable political genius of the present age, has scarcely ever wavered in his simple affection for his Prince and Princess of Orange, and though this affection is personal, not political—for nothing is political to the "man in the street"—there it is none the less, and it does not give way to either reasoning or prejudice.

Such is the external side of Court life. Internally it strikes one as simple and unaffected. Queen Emma was a lady possessing high qualifications as a mother and as a ruler. She grasped with undeniable shrewdness the popular taste and fancy; she had no difficulty in realising that her rather easy-going, sometimes blustering, Consort could have retained a great deal more of his popularity by very simple means, if he had cared to do so. She did care, so she allowed her little girl to be a little girl, and she let the people notice it. She went about with her, all through the country, and the people beheld not two proud princesses, strutting about in high and mighty manner, but a gracious, kind lady and an unaffected child. This child showed a genuine interest in sport in Friesland, in excavations in Maestricht, in ships and quays and docks in Rotterdam and Amsterdam, and in hospitals and orphanages everywhere. Anecdotes came into existence—the little Queen had been seen at "hop-scotch," had refused to go to bed early, had annoyed her governess, had been skating,

Court and Society

had been snow-balling her royal mother, etc. And later, when she was driving or riding, when she attended State functions or paid official visits, there was always a simplicity in her turn-out, a quiet dignity in her demeanour, which proved that she felt no particular desire to advertise herself as one of the wealthiest sovereigns of the world by the mere splendour of her surroundings.

This supreme tact of Queen Emma resulted in her daughter being educated as a queen as the Dutch like their sovereigns. Court life in The Hague or at the Loo certainly lacks neither dignity nor brilliancy, but it lacks showiness, and many an English nobleman lives in a grander style than Holland's Queen. Now, education may bend, but it does not alter a character, and whatever qualities may have adorned or otherwise influenced the late King, he was no more a stickler for etiquette or a lover of display than Queen Emma has proved to be. So there is a probability that their daughter will also be satisfied with very limited show, and if Prince Henry be wise, he will not interfere with the Queen's inclinations. He is said to be "horsy," but the same may be said of her, though as yet her "horsiness" has not become an absorbing passion, nor is it likely to be.

It is said also that she abhors music, but as long as she, as Queen, does not transfer her abhorrence from the art to the artists, no harm will be done. The facts are that, simple as her tastes are, she does not impose her simplicity upon others. When she presides at State dinners or at Court dinners, she is entirely the *grande dame*, but when she is allowed to be wholly herself, in a small, quiet circle, she is praised by everyone, low or high, who has been favoured with an invitation to the royal table, for her natural and unaffected manners, her urbanity, and her gentle courtesy.

CHAPTER III

THE PROFESSIONAL CLASSES

THE professional classes of Holland show their characteristics best in the social circle in which they move and find their most congenial companionships. Imagine, then, that we are the guests of the charming wife of a successful counsel (*advocaat en procureur*)—Mr. Walraven, let us call him—settled in a large and prosperous provincial town. She is a typical Dutch lady, with bright complexion, kind, clear blue eyes, rather dark eyebrows, which give a piquant air to the white and pink of the face, and a mass of fair golden hair, simply but tastefully arranged, leaving the ears free, and adorning but not hiding the comely shape of the head. She wears a dark-brown silk dress, covered with fine Brussels lace around the neck, at the wrists, along the bodice, and here and there on the skirt. A few rings glitter on her fingers, and her hands are constantly busy with a piece of point-lace embroidery; for many Dutch ladies cannot stand an evening without the companionship of a *handwerkje*, as fancy-needlework is called. It does not in the least interfere with their conversational duties. She is rather tall. Dutch men and women seem to have all sizes equally distributed amongst them ; it cannot be said that they are a short people, like the French and the Belgians, nor can the indication of middle-size be so rightly applied to them as to their German neighbours, whereas the taller Anglo-Saxons can frequently find their match in the Netherlands.

The room in which we are seated is furnished in so-called " old Dutch style." My friend and his wife have collected fine old wainscots, sideboards and cupboards of richly carved oak in Friesland and in the Flemish parts of Belgium. Their tables and chairs are all of the same material and artistically cut. A very dark, greenish-grey paper covers the walls ; the curtains, the carpet, and the doors are in the same slightly sombre shades. Venetian mirrors, Delft, Chinese and Rouen china plates, arranged along the walls, over the carved oak bench, and on the overmantel, make delightful patches of bright colour in the room, and the easy-chairs are as stylish as they are comfortable.

Our visit has fallen in the late autumn, and the gas burns brightly in the bronze chandelier, while the fire in the old-fashioned circulating stove, a rare specimen of ancient Flemish design, makes the room look cosy and hospitable. For the moment our friend the lawyer is absent. He has been called away to his study, for a client has come to see him on urgent business, and we are left in the gracious society of his wife in the comfortable sitting-room. On the table the Japan tray, with its silver teapot, sugar-basin, milk-jug, and spoon-box of mother-of-pearl and crystal, and its dark-blue real China cups and saucers, enjoys the company of two silver boxes, on silver trays, full of all sorts of *koekjes* (sweet biscuits). Many Dutch families like to take a *koekje* with their tea, tea-time falling in Holland between 7 and 8 o'clock, half-way between dinner at 5 or 6 P.M. and supper at 10 or 11 P.M. A cigar-stand is not wanting, nor yet dainty ashtrays; while by the side of our hostess is an old-fashioned brass *komfoor* or chafer,[1] on a high foot, so that within easy reach of the lady's hand is the handle of the brass kettle, in which the *theewater* is boiling.

Conversation turns from politics and literature to the ball to which my hostess, her husband, and we as their guests have been invited at a friend's house. She intends to go earlier; he and we are to follow later in the evening, for that evening his *Krans* is to meet at his house, and it will keep us till eleven o'clock. A *Krans* is simply a small company of very good friends who meet, as a rule, once a month, at the house of one of them, and at such meetings converse about

[1] *Komfoor* (or *kaffoor*) and *chafer* are etymologically the same word, derived from the Latin *calefacere*. The French member of the family is *chauffoir*.

things in general. The English word for *Krans* is "wreath," and the name indicates the intimate and thoroughly friendly relations existing between the composing members. They are twisted and twined together not merely by affectionate feeling, but also by equality of social position, education, and intelligence.

Our friends' little circle numbers seven, and as everyone of them happens to be the leading man in his profession in that town, and in consequence wields a powerful influence, their *Krans* is generally nicknamed the "Heptarchy." Our friend the lawyer is not only a popular legal adviser, but as *Wethouder* (alderman) for finance and public works he is the much-admired originator of the rejuvenated town. The place had been fortified in former days, but after the home defence of Holland was reorganised and a system of defence on a coherent and logically conceived basis accepted, all fortified towns disappeared and became open cities, of which this was one. The public-spirited lawyer grasped the situation at once, and, spurred by his influence and enthusiasm, the Town Council adopted a large scheme of streets, roads, parks, and squares, so that when all was completed the inhabitants of the old city scarcely knew where they were. Besides this, he is legal adviser of the local branch of the Netherlands Bank, a director on the boards of various limited companies, and the president-director of a prosperous Savings Bank.

The Professional Classes

Nevertheless, he finds time in his crowded life to read a great deal, to see his friends occasionally, and to keep up an incessant courtship of his handsome wife, who in return asseverates that he is the most sociable husband in the world.

After Walraven has returned to the tea-table, his admiring consort leaves us, and shortly afterwards his best friend, within and without the *Krans*, Dr. Klaassen, appears on the scene. He and Dr. Klaassen were students at the same University, and nothing is better fitted to form lifelong friendship than the freedom of Holland's University life and University education. Dr. Klaassen is one of the most attractive types of the Dutch medical man. His University examinations did not tie him too tightly to his special science. Like all Dutch students, he mixed freely with future lawyers, clergymen, philosophers, and philologists, and it is often said that while the University teaches young men chiefly sound methods of work, students in Holland acquire quite as much instruction from each other as from their professors. Doctor Klaassen left the University as fresh as when he entered it, and ready to take a healthy interest in all departments of human affairs. He is a man to whom the Homeric phrase might well be applied—"A physician is a man knowing more than many others."

His non-professional work takes him to the boards and committees of societies promoting charity, ethics, religion, literature, and the fine arts. The local branch of the famous *Maatschappij tot Nut van 't Algemeen* (the " Society for promoting the Common-weal ") and its various institutions, schools, libraries, etc., find in him one of their most energetic and faithful directors; a local hospital admitting people of all religious denominations has grown up by his untiring energy; and he prepared the basis upon which younger men afterwards built what is now a model institution in Holland ; nor does he forget the poor and the orphans, to whom he gives quite half his time, though how much of his money he gives them nobody knows, least of all he himself.

The Reverend Mr. Barendsen, the third arrival, is a very different person. His sermons are eloquent; he is a fluent speaker—too fluent, some say, for words and phrases come so easily to him that the lack of thought is not always felt by this preacher, although noticed by his flock. Now, a sermon for Dutch Protestants is a difficult thing; it has to be long enough to fill nearly a whole service of about two hours ; and it is listened to by educated and uneducated people, who all expect to be edified. Domine Barendsen, like so many of his colleagues, tries to meet this difficulty by giving light nourishment in an attractive form. But if his sermons do not succeed as well as his kind intentions deserve, his influence is firmly established by his sympathetic personality.

The Professional Classes

He may be much more superficial than his two friends; he may be less dogged, less tenacious than they; yet his fertile brain, his quick intelligence, and his serious character have won for him a unique position, and his public influence is very great. Both doctor and parson meet and mix in the best society of the town, but the slums of the poor are also equally well known to them; neither is a member of the Town Council, but the same institutions have their common support. Livings in Holland are not over-luxurious; and the consequence is that many "domines" go out lecturing, or make an additional income by translating or writing books. Some of Holland's best and most successful authors and poets are, or were, clergymen, such as Allard Pierson, P. A. de Genestet, Nicolaas Beets (Hildebrand), Coenraad Busken Huet, J. J. L. ten Kate, Dr. Jan ten Brink, Bernard ter Haar, etc. Domine Barendsen is likewise well known in Dutch literary circles.

General Hendriks is the next to be announced. Dutch officers do not like to go about in their uniform, but the gallant general is also expected at the ball, and so he has donned his military garments. He is a *Genist* a Royal Engineer, and had his education at the Royal Military Academy at Breda. This means that he is no swashbuckler, but a genial, well-mannered, open-minded, and well-read gentleman, with a somewhat scientific turn of mind and a rare freedom from military prejudice. Hollanders are not a military people in the German sense, and fire-eaters and military fanatics are rare, but they are rarest amongst the officers of the General Staff, the Royal Engineers, and the Artillery.

General Hendriks married a lady of title with a large fortune, so his position is a very pleasant one. His friendship for the other "Heptarchists" is necessarily of recent date, for he has been abroad a great deal, and was five years in the Dutch East Indies fighting in the endless war against Atchin. His stay there has widened his views still more, and when he tells of his experiences he is at once interesting and attractive, for he is well-informed and a charming *raconteur*. His rank causes society to impose on him duties which he is inclined to consider as annoying, but he fulfils them graciously enough. He is a popular president-director of the *Groote Societeit* (the Great Club), and of Cæcilia, the most prominent society for vocal and instrumental music; and whenever races, competitions, exhibitions, bazaars, and similar social functions, to which the Dutch are greatly addicted, take place, General Hendriks is sure to be one of the honorary presidents, or at least a member of the working board, and his urbanity and affability are certain to ensure success. He has been a member of the States-General, and is said to be a probable future Minister of War. But the weak spot in his heart is for poetry and for literature generally ; the number of poems he knows by heart is marvellous, and at the meetings of the Heptarchy he freely indulges his love of quotations, a pleasure he strictly denies himself in other surroundings, for fear of boring people. But everybody has a dim presumption that the General knows a good deal more than most people are aware of, and this dim presumption is strengthened by the very firm conviction that he is an exceedingly genial man and a "jolly good fellow."

Mr. Ariëns, Lit. D., "Rector" of the Gymnasium (equivalent to Head-master of a Grammar School), is the most remarkable type even in this very remarkable set of men. He is highly unconventional, and his boys adore him, while his old boys admire him, and the parents are his perennial debtors in gratitude. He is unconventional in everything,—in his dress, in his way of living, in his opinions and judgments; but he parades none of these, reducing them to neither a whim nor a hobby. He passed some years in the Dutch Indies, travelled all over Europe, knows more of Greek, Latin, and antiquities than anybody else, and is as thoroughly scientific as any University professor. But the Government will never give him a vacant chair, for his pedagogical powers surpass even his scientific abilities, and they cannot spare such men in such places. To some aristocratic people his noble simple-mindedness is downright appalling ; but when he goes about in dull, cold, wintry weather and visits the poor wretches in the slums, where nature and natural emotions and forms of speech are quite unconventional, he is duly appreciated. For he is not only a splendid *gymnasii rector;* he is also a very charitable man, though he likes only one form of charity, that by which the rich man first educates himself into being the poor man's friend, and then only offers his sympathy and help—the charity which the one can give and the other take without either of them feeling degraded by the act. He is not a public-body man, our "Rector," but his friends appreciate his keen, just judgment. They may disagree with him on some points, but a discussion with him is always interesting on account of his original, fresh method of thought, and instructive by reason of his very superior and universal knowledge.

His best friend is Mr. Jacobs, a civil engineer. Dutch civil engineers are educated at Delft, at the Polytechnic School, after having passed their final examination at a "Higher Burgher School." Boys of sixteen or seventeen are not fit to digest sciences by the dozen, and, however, pleasant and convenient it may be to become a walking cyclopedia, a cyclopedia is not a living book, but a dead accumulation of dead knowledge, which may inform though it does not educate. Happily, the majority of Dutch engineers are saved by the Polytechnic School, where they have about the same liberty as undergraduates at the Universities to go their own way. Educationally, they are not so well equipped, attention only being paid to mental instruction, for the Director of a " Higher Burgher School " is a different man from the Rector of a Gymnasium, while the system over which he presides is more or less incoherent, so far as educational considerations go.

But if a civil engineer is a success he is generally a big one. So is Mr. Jacobs. He is thoroughly well read, though his reading may be somewhat desultory. His splendid memory, assisted by a remarkably quick wit, allows him to feel interested in nearly everything — sociology, literature, art, music, theatre, sport, charity, municipal enterprise. If he is superficial, nobody notices it, for he is much too smart to show it. His general level-headedness makes him an inexhaustible source of admiration to Dr. Ariëns, whose peer he is in kindness of heart. His manner is irreproachable ; he never loses his temper in discussion, and treats his opponents in such a quiet, courteous way that they are obviously sorry to disagree with him. His business capacities are of the first rank; he makes as much money as he likes, and however crowded his life may be, he always finds time for more work. He is a member of the Town Council and a staunch supporter of Walraven's progressive plans. Walraven has certain misgivings about Jacobs' thoroughness, but he fully realises his friend's quick grasp of things. He may build bridges, irrigate whole districts, and drain marshes in Holland, open up mines in Spain, build docks in America, or hunt for petroleum in Russia ; he is always sure to succeed, and a fair profit for himself, at any rate, is the invariable result of his exertions. He travels a great deal, knows everybody everywhere, and always turns up again in the old haunts, bristling with interesting information, visibly enjoying his busy, full life, and not without a certain vanity, arising from the feeling that his fellow-citizens are rather proud of him.

The last to come is Mr. Smits, President of the Court of Justice, a man of philosophical turn of mind, an ardent student of social problems, a fine lawyer, a first-rate speaker, a shrewd judge of men, and a tolerant and mild critic of their weaknesses. He also is a member of the Town Council, and, like Jacobs, a member of a municipal committee of which Walraven is the chairman. Their duties are the supervision and general management of the communal trade and industry, such as tramways, gas-works, water-supply, slaughter-houses, electrical supply, corn exchange, public parks and public gardens, hot-houses and plantations, etc. Smits is also the chairman of two debating societies, one for workmen and the other for the better educated classes; but social problems are the chief topics discussed at both. These societies, he says, keep him well

The Professional Classes

in touch with the general drift of the popular mind; as a fact, by his encouraging ways, he draws from the people what is in their thoughts and hearts, and very often succeeds in correcting wrong impressions and conceptions. He is also the Worshipful Master of the local Masonic lodge, "The Three Rings," so-called after the famous parable of religious tolerance in Lessing's noble drama, *Nathan der Weise*. Dutch Freemasonry is not churchy as in England; it is charitable, teaches ethics as distinct from, but not opposed to, religion, admits men of all creeds and of no creed whatever, and preaches tolerance all round; but it fights indifferentism, apathy, or carelessness on all matters affecting the material, intellectual, and psychical well-being of mankind.

Smits feels very strongly on all these matters, and his enthusiasm is of a staying kind; but the ancient device *Suaviter in modo* has quite as much charm for him as its counterpart, *Fortiter in re*. The consequence is that superficial people take him for a Socialist because he neither prosecutes nor persecutes Socialists for the opinions they hold. Himself an agnostic, and lacking religious sentiment, he realises so well the supreme influence of religion on numberless people and the comfort they derive from it, that many consider him not nearly firm enough in his intercourse with Roman Catholics or "orthodox" Protestants, with whom, in fact, he frequently arranges political "deals." For Smits is, if not the chairman, the most influential and active member of the Liberal caucus ; and, being in favour of proportional representation, he insists that the other political parties shall have their fair number of Town Councillors.

Such are the men who come together in this elegant and yet homely sitting-room ; each of them a leader in his profession, each of them coming in daily and close contact with all sorts and conditions of men and women in the town, and enabled by their wide and unbiassed views of humanity and human affairs to control them and to divert the common energies into wise paths. The "Heptarchy" has, of course, no legal standing as such, but from their conversations one understands the influence which its members wield by their intellectual and moral superiority. They conspire in no way to attain certain ends, but discuss things as intimately as only brothers or man and wife can discuss them, in the genial intimacy of their unselfish friendship. They generally agree on the lines to be taken in certain matters, but even if they fail to agree, this does not prevent them from acting according to their own lights, still respecting each other's convictions and preferences. And not only local topics are discussed in the meetings of the "Heptarchy," but politics, art, trade, and science, foreign and Dutch, come within their scope ; for their intellectual outlook, like their sympathies, is universal.

The Professional Classes

Towards eleven o'clock we take leave of each other, Walraven, Hendriks, and ourselves go to the ball at the house of the *Commissaris der Koningin* (Queen's Commissioner), the Lord-Lieutenant of the County, Baron Alma van Strae. Baron and Baroness Alma live in a palatial mansion, and we find the huge reception and drawing rooms full of a gay crowd of young folk. The rooms are beautifully decorated: there is a profusion of flowers and palms in the halls and on the stairs; and a host of footmen, in bright-buttoned, buff-coloured livery coats, short trousers, and white stockings, move quietly about, betraying the well-trained instincts of hereditary lackeydom. There are county councillors, judges, officers of army and navy, bankers, merchants, manufacturers, town councillors, the mayor and town clerk, the president and some members of the Chamber of Commerce, and committee-men of orphanages and homes for old people. All have brought their wives, daughters, and sons to do the dancing, for though they occasionally join themselves, they prefer to indulge in a quiet game of whist or to settle down in Baron Alma's smoking and billiard room for a cigar.

These social functions, however, are much the same in Holland as in other countries. Etiquette may differ in small details, but on the whole the world of society lives the same life, cultivates the same interests, and amuses or bores itself in much the same fashion. It is *tout comme chez nous* in this as in nearly everything else.

On the whole, this elegant crowd shows a somewhat greater amount of deference towards professionals than towards officials. Doctors, lawyers, and parsons are clearly highly esteemed; it is the victory of intellect in a fair field of encounter. In The Hague the officials beat them, but not so much on account of their office as in consequence of the fact that so many are titled persons, highly connected and frequently well off. But after the great Revolution and the Napoleonic times, officialdom lost its influence and social importance in Holland in consequence of the demolition of the oligarchic, patrician Republic ; and Clause 5 of the Netherlands Constitution, which declares that " Every Netherlander may be appointed to every public office," is a very real and true description of the actual, visible facts of social life.

CHAPTER IV

THE POSITION OF WOMEN

THE Dutchwoman, generally speaking, is not the "new woman," in the sense of taking any very definite part in the politics of the country. Neither does she interest herself in, nor interfere in, ecclesiastical matters. Dutchmen have not a very high opinion of the mental and administrative qualities of their womenfolk outside of what is considered their sphere, but for all that the women of the upper class are certainly more clever than the men, but as they do not take any practical part in the questions which are "burning," as far as any question does burn in this land of dampness, their interest is academic rather than real. The wives of the small shopkeeper, the artisan, and the peasant take much the same place as women of these classes in other European countries. They are kind mothers, thrifty housewives, very fond of their "man," not averse to the fascinations of dress, and in their persons and houses extremely trim and tidy, while the poorest quarters of the large towns are, compared with the slums of London, Manchester, and Liverpool, pictures of neatness. It is true that windows are seldom opened, for no Dutch window opens at the top, and so in passing by an open door in the poor quarters of a town one gets a whiff of an inside atmosphere which baffles description; but the inside of the house is "tidy," and one can see the gleam of polished things, telling of repeated rubbings, scrubbings, and scourings. In fact, cleanliness in Holland has become almost a disease, and scrubbing and banging go on from morning until night both outside and inside a house.

Probably the abundant supply of water accounts for the universal washing, for, not content with washing everything inside a house, they wash the outside too, and even the bark of any trees which happen to lie within the zone of operations. The plinths and bricks of the houses are scrubbed as far as the arms can reach or a little hand-squirt can carry water. In cottages both in town and country there is the same cleanliness, but the people stop short of washing themselves, and the bath among the poorer classes is practically unknown. People of this kind may not have had one for thirty or forty years, and will receive the idea with derision and look on the practice as a "fad," while the case of many animals is seriously cited as an argument that it is quite unnecessary. A doctor told me once of a rich old patient of the farming class near Utrecht who, on being ordered a bath, said:

ZEELAND COSTUMES

"Any amount of physic, but a bath—never!" On the principle that you cannot do everything, personal cleanliness is apt to go to the wall, and the energies of the Dutchwomen of the lower middle and the poorer classes are concentrated on washing everything *inanimate*, even the brick footpath before the houses, which accounts for the clean appearance of the Dutch streets in town and country. Even a heavy downpour of rain does not interfere with the housewife's or servant's weekly practice, and you will see servants holding up umbrellas while they wash the fronts of the houses. This excessive cleanliness, together with the other household duties of mother and wife, fills up the ordinary day, and a newspaper or book is seldom seen in their hands.

Passing on to the middle class, we find the mistress's time largely taken up with directing the servants and bargaining with the tradesmen, who in many cases bring their goods round from house to house. The lady of the house takes care to lock up everything after the supplies for the day have been given out, and the little basket full of keys which she carries about with her is a study in itself. Even in the upper class this locking up is a general practice, for very few people keep a housekeeper. The mistress also takes care of the "pot." This is an ingenious but objectionable device to make a guest pay for his dinner. On leaving a house after dining you give one of the servants a florin, and all the money so collected is put into a box, and at certain times is divided between the servants, so that a servant on applying for a situation asks what is the value of the " pot " in the year. There are signs of this practice of feeing servants after a dinner being done away with, for it spoils the idea of hospitality, and one's host on bidding you " Good-bye " resorts to many little artifices in order not to see that you do fee his servant, added to which you are very likely to shake hands with him with the florin in your hand, which you have been furtively trying to transfer to the left hand from the right, and very often the guest drops the wretched coin in his efforts to give it unseen. It is to be hoped that the ladies of Holland will succeed in abolishing a custom which is disagreeable alike to entertainer and entertained.

The women of the upper middle class are certainly much better educated than their English sisters. They always can speak another language than their own, and very often two, French and English now being common, while a few add German and a little Italian, but most of them read German, if they do not speak it. French is universal, however, for the French novel is far more to the taste than the more sober English book. The number and quality of these French books read by the Dutch young lady are enough to astonish and probably shock an English girl, who reads often with difficulty the safe " Daudet "

(*Sapho* excepted), but the young Dutchwoman knows of no *Index Expurgatorius*, and reads what she likes. At the same time, the classics of England and Germany are very generally read and valued, and many a Dutchwoman could pass a better examination on the text and meaning of Shakespeare than the Englishwoman, whose knowledge is too often limited to memories of the Cambridge texts of the great poets used in schools.

But, well educated as the Dutchwoman undoubtedly is, there is nothing about her of the "blue-stocking," and she does not impress you as being clever until a long acquaintance has brought out her many-sided knowledge. The great pity is that her education leads to so little, for there are very few channels into which a Dutchwoman can direct her knowledge. Politics turn for the most part on differences in religious questions, which are abstruse and dry to the feminine mind, and of practical political life she sees nothing. There is no "terrace," no Primrose League, no canvassing, no political *salon*, no excitement about elections; and, added to these negatives, women get snubbed if they venture opinions on political matters, and young people generally look upon politics *et hoc genus omne* as a bore, and the names of great statesmen at the helm of affairs are frequently not even known by the younger generation. Little interest is also taken in the army and navy, owing to the fact that there is so little active service in the former and to the smallness of the latter; and woman does not care much about orders, regulations, manœuvres, and comparative strength;—she wants "heroes," and to know what they have done, and does not consider what the "services" might, could, or should do. The officers who have served in India and have seen active service rank high in her estimation, but as these are few, beyond the affection bestowed upon soldier husband, brother, or lover, which is chiefly displayed in anxiety lest they should be sent to do garrison duty in some town where social advantages are small or *nil*, there is no great interest taken in army affairs by the Dutchwoman. As to the navy, they philosophically acquiesce in the fact that as a ship must sail on the water they must patiently bear the necessary separation from their sailor friends.

When we come to things ecclesiastical, there is still less interest taken in the Church. The Roman Catholic Church is outside the question, for the position of the laity there has been well described as "kneeling in front of the altar, sitting under the pulpit, and putting one's hand in one's pocket without demur when money is required." The Protestant laity, however, do not take any great interest in the National Church, and while there are deaconesses devoted to nursing, and all good works, as there are *sœurs de charité* in the Roman communion, yet the rank and file of Dutchwomen do not trouble about

The Position of Women

their church beyond attending it occasionally—one may say, very occasionally. There is but little brightness in the services of the Reformed Church,—no ritual, no scope for artistic work, no curates, and above and beyond all, no career in the Church for the clergy. At the best, they may get sent to one of the large towns, but the life is the same as in the village for the wife of the "domine," as the Dutch pastor is called. And if the "domines" move about in fear and trembling because of the argus-eyes and often Midas-like ears of the deacons, their wives must be still more discreet. One "domine" has been known to brave public opinion and ride a bicycle, but for a mother in Israel to do the like would scandalise all good members of the Reformed Church. The wives of the clergy, however, do good and useful work, and probably are more real helpmeets to their husbands than women in any other class of what may be called official life, but they take no sort of lead in parochial or ecclesiastical matters. They do not direct the feminine influences which do work in the parish, but rather take their place as one of them. If, therefore, a woman marries a clergyman, she does so for love of the man and his work's sake; there cannot be a tinge of ambition as to the career of her husband, for there are no such things as comfortable rectories and prospective deaneries or bishoprics, with their consequent influence and power. Nothing but love of the man brings the "domine" a wife, and she knows that there will be inquisitorial eyes and not too kind speeches about her behaviour from the "faithful," while the great people, to their loss, will ignore her socially in much the same way as Queen Elizabeth did the wives of the bishops in her day.

Passing to lighter subjects, Dutch girls are now breaking loose from the stiffness and espionage in which their mothers were brought up, and this is without doubt in a large measure due to the introduction of sport. Tennis, hockey, golf, and more especially bicycling, have conferred, by the force of circumstances, a freedom which strength of argument, entreaty, and tears failed to effect. Mothers and chaperones do not, as a rule, bicycle, and play tennis and golf; they cannot always go to club meetings, even to yawn through the sets, and so the young people play by themselves, and there are fast growing a lack of restraint and a healthy freedom of intercourse which are gravely deprecated by grandmammas, winked at by mothers, but enjoyed to the full by daughters. But quidnuncs prophesy, however, that people will not marry as early as of yore, for young people get to know one another too well by unrestricted intercourse, and the halo with which each sex surrounds the other is dispelled. Be this as it may, no Dutch girl wishes to go back to the old days when she could go nowhere alone.

Yet, however much men like to have women as companions in games, they are not so willing to

The Position of Women

allow them much to say in matters which the masculine mind considers its own province; for the fact is that most Dutchmen consider women inferiors, and when there is a question of admittance into literary or artistic circles and clubs, women's work has to be of an undeniably high order. There are one or two ladies' clubs, but they do not at present flourish, there being so few public platforms on which women can meet, and so the " social grade " determines women's relative position by women's votes, and there is small chance of crossing the Rubicon then. There is no doubt, however, that women in Holland are slowly winning their way to greater independence of life. They are filling posts in public offices; they are going to the universities; they are studying medicine and qualifying as doctors; and no doubt they will in time compel men to acknowledge their claims to live an independent life rather than a dependent one.

Besides, in Holland, as in other countries, the proportion between the sexes is unequal, and so necessity will force open doors of usefulness hitherto closed to women.

The Dutchwoman dresses expensively in all the towns, and generally well. The toilettes are mostly of a German model, which suits the build of the Dutchwoman better than the fashions of Paris. Rarely, however, do women dress in that simple style in vogue in English morning dress, and a Dutch town or seaside resort is filled in the

mornings with gay toilettes more fitted for the
Row or the Boulevard. Even when bicycling,
the majority do not dress very simply.

Holland has always been noted for the variety
and quaintness of its provincial and even communal costumes, and these may all still be seen,
though they are dying out slowly. In some,
and in fact many cases, a modern bonnet is
worn over a beautiful gold or silver headpiece,
fringed with lace, but ancient and modern do not
in such cases harmonise. Of the distinctly provincial costumes, that of Friesland is generally
considered the prettiest, but as illustrations are
given of them all in a later chapter, it must be
left to the reader to decide the point for himself.
The fisherfolk, more than any other, retain their
distinctive dress, although even among them
some of the children are habited according to
modern ideas, and certainly when the women are
doomed to wear fourteen or sixteen skirts, which
has the effect of making them liable to pulmonary
complaints, it is surprising that modern fashions
are not more generally adopted. The plea for
modernity in respect to Dutch national costumes
is considered rank heresy among artists, but the
figures look better in a picture and at a distance
than in everyday life, added to which the custom
of cutting off or hiding the hair, which some of
the head-dresses compel, is not one to be encouraged; and it is a wonder that woman, who knows
as a rule her charms, has for so long consented to

DUTCH FISHER-GIRLS

The Position of Women

be deprived of one of the chief ones. But in Holland, as in all countries where education is spreading, cosmopolitanism in dress is increasing, and the picturesque tends to give place to the convenient and in many cases the healthy.

Marriage, with all its preliminaries, is woman's triumph, and in Holland she makes the most of it. The manner of seeking a wife and proposing is no doubt the same in the Netherlands as in other European countries, with the exception of France, but, once accepted, the happy man must resign himself to the accustomed routine. First of all, he exchanges rings, so that a man who is engaged or married betrays the fact as well as a woman by a plain gold ring worn on the third finger. A girl, therefore, has a better chance against those who were "deceivers ever" than in a country where no such outward and visible sign exists. The engagement is announced by cards being sent out, countersigned by the parents on both sides, and a day is fixed for receiving the congratulations. The betrothed are then considered almost married. Engagements are, of course, frequently broken off, but such a thing as an action for "breach of promise" is impossible, and would be considered most mercenary and mean. As a rule, engagements are not long, and as soon as the wedding-day is agreed upon, the preceding fortnight is filled with parties of various kinds, while there is another great reception just before the wedding-day, in which, as before, the bride and bridegroom have to stand for hours receiving the congratulations of their friends. Every now and then they will snatch a chance to sit down, but another arrival brings them again to their feet, weary but smiling. On the wedding morning the happy couple drive to the Town Hall ; for all marriages must first be celebrated by the civil authorities, and so they appear before their Burgomaster, who says something appropriate, and they make their vows and sign the papers, after which, if they desire it, there is a service at the church which is called a "Benediction," at which they are blessed, and have to listen to a long sermon, at the close of which a Bible is given them. This sermon is not the least of the trying experiences, for frequently many of the older members of the party are reduced to tears by allusions to former members of the two families, and all sorts of subjects alien to the particular service are introduced. At a recent wedding, known to me, the guests had to listen to a long address in which the Transvaal War and the Paris Exhibition were commented upon. Not only so, but no fewer than three collections are taken at the service, so that people who desire to enter into the holy estate of matrimony must not lack fortitude when they have made up their minds to it.

But, once married, a Dutch home is indeed "Home, sweet home," as is the case more or less in all the northern countries, where the changeful climate compels people to live a great deal within four walls. Dutch fathers are kind, and the mothers are indulgent, and, among the poorer classes especially, family affection is very great. Most beautiful and touching instances might be abundantly quoted of family devotion, and a society like that for the " prevention of cruelty to children " would find little to do in Holland.

CHAPTER V

THE WORKMAN OF THE TOWNS

THE condition of the Dutch urban working classes is by no means an enviable one. Granting that wages are much higher than half a century ago, when bread cost fivepence-halfpenny the loaf as against three halfpence to-day, and when clothes and furniture cost fifty per cent. more than now, the average working-man cannot be otherwise described than as distinctly poor when compared with his English colleague. Yet it would be misleading to judge exclusively by the scale of wages, and against making comparisons of the kind the reader should at once be warned. The fact is that there are very wide divergences of condition amongst the working classes of Holland. A carpenter or a blacksmith earning from £1 to £1 10s. in weekly wages all the year round will rank, if sober and well-behaved, as a comparatively well-to-do workman. On the other hand, a bricklayer or a painter, whose work in winter is very uncertain, and who earns, maybe, a bare £1 a week during the nine months of the year wherein he can find work, is a poor workman at the best, and his condition is greatly to be deplored. More pitiable still, however, is the case of working-class families in some of the manufacturing towns, where wages are still lower, and where an even tolerable standard of life cannot be maintained unless mother and children take their place in the factory side by side with the head of the household as regular wage-earners.

For, as labour is cheap and families are numerous in Holland, as soon as the boys and girls have reached the sacramental age of twelve, at which Dutch law allows them to work twelve hours a day, they leave school, and enter the factory and workshop.

It is no joke for these children, who have to leave their little beds, frequently under the tiles, at 5 or 6 A.M., or earlier, summer and winter, to gulp down some hot coffee, or what is conveniently called so, to swallow a huge piece of the well-known Dutch *roggebrood*, or rye-bread, and then to hurry, in their wooden shoes, through the quiet streets of the town to their place of work.

Sometimes they have time to return home at 8 or 8.30 A.M. for a second hurried "breakfast," which, as often as not, is their first, for many of them start the day's work on an empty stomach. Those who cannot run home and back in the half-hour usually allowed for the first *schaft*, or meal-time, take their bread-and-butter with them in a cotton or linen bag, and their milk-and-water or coffee in a tin, and so shift as well as they can. Dinner-time, as a rule, finds the whole family united from about twelve until one o'clock or half-past in the kitchen at home. This kitchen is, of course, used for cooking, washing, dwelling, and sleeping purposes. The walls are whitewashed, and the floor consists of flagstones. Of luxury, there is none; of comfort, little. Generally, the fare of the day is potatoes, with some other vegetable — carrots, turnips, cabbage, or beans. A piece of bacon, rarely beef, is sometimes added; while mutton is hardly ever eaten in Holland, unless by very poor people. Fish is too expensive for most of them, except fried kippers or bloaters. If there is time over, and the house has a little garden attached to it, the children help by watering the vegetables growing there, should it be summer-time, or by making themselves generally useful. But at 1 or 1.30 they have to be back at the workshop, and until 7 P.M. the drudgery goes on again. On Saturday evening the boy brings his sixpence, or whatever his trifling wages may be, to his mother. Rent and the club-money for illness and funeral expenses must be at hand when the collectors call either on Sunday or Monday morning. As a rule, though the exceptions are numerous enough, the father also brings his whole pay with him; but drink is the curse—a decreasing curse, it may be, but still a curse—of many a workman's family,

The Workman of the Towns

and in such cases the inroads it makes in the domestic budget are very serious.

So the boys grow up—in a busy, monotonous life—until they are called upon to subject themselves to compulsory military service. Before they become recruits, they have usually joined various societies — debating, theatrical, social, political, or other. Arnold Toynbee has a good many admirers and followers in Holland, who do yeoman's work after his spirit, and bring bright, healthy pleasure into the lives of these youthful toilers. Divines of all denominations, Protestant and Catholic, have also their "At homes" and their "Congregations," and innocent amusement is not unseldom mixed with religious teaching at their meetings. In this way, too, a helpful, restraining influence is exerted upon youth. And gradually the boy becomes a young man, associating with other young men, and, like his wealthier neighbours, discussing the world's affairs, dreaming of drastic reforms, and thinking less and less of the dreary home, where father and mother, grown old before their time, are little more than the people with whom he boards, and who take the whole or part of his wages, allowing him some modest pocket-money for himself.

In the meantime his sisters have been living with some middle-class family, starting as errand-girls, being afterwards promoted to the important position of *kindermeid*, or children's maid, though all the time sleeping out, which means that before and after having toiled a whole day for strangers, they do part of the housework for their mothers at home. After some time, however, they find employment as housemaids, or in other domestic positions. If they have the good fortune to find considerate yet strict and conscientious mistresses, the best time of their life now begins; there is no exhaustion from work, yet good food, good lodging, and kind treament. Should they care to cultivate the fine art of cooking, they get instruction in that line, and are in most cases allowed to work independently, and even, when reliable and trustworthy, to do the buying of vegetables, etc., by themselves in the market-places, which all Dutch towns boast of, and in which the produce of the land is offered for sale in abundance and appetising freshness. All this tends to teach a servant-girl how to use alike her eyes, hands, and brain, and to educate her into a thrifty, industrious, and tidy workman's wife, who will know how to make both ends meet, however short her resources may be. This is one of the reasons why so many Dutch workmen's homes, notwithstanding the low wages, have an appearance of snug prosperity—the women there have learned how to make a little go a long way.

And how about their future husbands? Have they, too, learned their trade? Perhaps; if they are particularly strong, shrewd, industrious, and persevering, though technical education (*ambachtsonderwys*) is much a thing of the future in Holland.

In the general course of life a boy goes to a trade which offers him the highest wages. If he can begin by earning eightpence a week, he will not go elsewhere to earn sixpence if the wear and tear of shoes and clothes is the same in both cases, although the sixpenny occupation may perhaps be better suited to his tastes, ability, and general aptitude. To his mother the extra two pence are a consideration; they may cover some weekly contribution to a necessary fund. Running errands is his first work, until accidentally some workman or some apprentice leaves the shop, in which case he is moved up, and a new boy has the errands to do. But now he must look out for himself; his master is not over-anxious to let him learn all the ins and outs of the work, for as soon as his competitors hear that he has a very clever boy in his shop, he is sure to lose that boy, who is tempted away by the offer of better pay. Nor are the workmen greatly inclined to impart their little secrets, to explain this thing and that, and so help the young fellow on. Why should they? Nobody did it for them; they got their qualifications by their own unaided exertions — let the boy do the same. Moreover, the *baas* or chief, does not like them to " waste their time " in that manner, and the *baas* is the dispenser of their bread and butter;

so the boy is, as a rule, regarded merely as a nuisance.

There are workshops, first-class workshops, too, where no apprentices have been admitted for dozens of years, simply because the employers do not see their way to make an efficient agreement with the boys or their parents which would prevent them from letting a competitor enjoy the results of their technical instruction. One would not be astonished that in these circumstances all over Holland the want of technical schools is badly felt, and that agitation for their provision is active. Only some twenty-four such schools exist at present; the oldest, that at Amsterdam, dates from 1861, and the youngest, that of Nymegen, was established in 1890. Partly municipal schools, partly schools built by the private effort of citizens, they all do their work well. It is only during the last few years that the nation has begun to ask whether technical education ought not to be taken up by the State. The Dutch like private enterprise in everything, and are always inclined to prefer it to State or municipal action; but they have come to recognise that technical schools may be good schools, and may do good work on behalf of the much-needed improvement of handicraft, even though not private ventures, and that so far this branch of national education has not kept up with the times.

The idea which will probably in the end gain

The Workman of the Towns 57

the day, is that the technical schools should be managed by the Town Councils and subsidised by the State, who in return would receive the right of supervision and inspection, and of laying down general rules for their curricula. For the present, however, there is no law settling the question, and the apprentices are the sufferers by the lack, since the employers shrink from employing their means, time, and knowledge on behalf of unscrupulous competitors.

In general the life of an urban workingman is a constant struggle against poverty and sickness. Children come plentifully, rather too much so for the inelastic possibilities of their parents' wages. The young wife does not get stronger by frequent confinements; and the fare is bound to get less nourishing as the mouths round the domestic board increase — always simple, it often becomes insufficient. The mother, working hard already, has to work harder still and to do laundry work at home or go out as a charwoman, in order to increase the modest income. In industrial centres women frequently work in the factories as well, though the law does at least protect them against too long hours and premature work after confinement.

Thanks to the Dutch thrift, burial funds and sickness funds come promptly to the rescue when death lays his iron grip on the wasted form of the poor town-bred babies, when illness saps the man's power to earn his usual wages, and the family's income is for the time cut off. Of these benefit funds there are about 450 in Holland, distributed amongst some 150 towns. Half of them are burial funds, and half mixed burial and sickness funds ; their members number about two millions ; yet, although they certainly do much to prevent extreme poverty, they do it in a manner which in many cases is little short of a scandal. Their legal status is rather uncertain, and in consequence many managers do as they like, and make a good thing for themselves out of their duty to the poor. Too often these managers are supreme controllers of the funds, and the members have no influence whatever. In many cases the only official the latter know is the collector, who calls at their houses for the weekly contributions. This official frequently resorts to questionable tricks for extorting money from the poor helpless members, who simply and confidently pay what they are told to pay—small sums, of course, a few cents or pence, it may be, but still " adding up " in the long run—and when sorrow and death enter their humble dwellings they are easily imposed upon by cool scoundrels, who trade on their disinclination to quarrel about money when there is a corpse in the house.

Another danger of the irregular condition of these funds lies in the fact that outsiders may take out policies on the lives of certain families. A few years ago the country was shocked by the alarming story of a woman who had poisoned a

AN OVERYSSEL FARMHOUSE

The Workman of the Towns

series of persons merely to be able to get the funeral expenses paid to herself, while many a wretched little baby has in this manner been the horrible investment of heartless neighbours, who, knowing the poor thing was dying, took out policies for its funeral. For medical examination is not required for these beautifully managed associations. Their premiums are, however, so high that this detail does not materially affect their sound financial position; and this being the case, it cannot be denied that the absence of such examinations considerably increases their general utility for the labouring classes.

The clubs for preventing financial loss by illness do require a medical examination. They number in Holland nearly 700, distributed in over 300 towns. Some allow a fixed sum of money during illness, others provide doctor and medicines, others do both. But the same objections and grievances which workmen entertain against burial funds apply likewise to these latter clubs. The curious thing is that, instead of grumbling, the workman does not make up his mind to mend matters by insisting on having a share in the management of societies and funds to which he has contributed so large a part of his earnings. As yet, however, the Dutch labouring classes have not found the man who is able to organise them for this or other purposes. They have able advocates, eloquent, passionate reformers, straightforward, honest friends, but the work of these is more destructive criticism than constructive organisation. Where organisation exists, it is political, social, religious, but not industrial—local, but not universal, and it often has the bitter suggestion of charity. On the other hand, the poor fellows have so often been imposed upon that they feel very little confidence in each other and in the wealthier classes who profess deep interest in their woes and sorrows. There are no very large industrial centres in Holland ; the wages are so low that most workmen are obliged to find supplementary incomes, either by doing overtime, or by doing odd jobs after the regular day's work is over. Hence there is not much time or energy left for the common cause. Some great employers, like Mr. J. C. van Marken, of Delft, and Messrs. Stork Brothers of Hengeloo, have organisations of their own, by which important ameliorations are obtained ; but smaller employers hear the labour leaders constantly deprecating such efforts and preaching the blessings of Social Democracy as the true panacea, so they do not see why they should put themselves to any inconvenience or expense for the sake of earning abuse and ingratitude.

Moreover, many of these employers adhere to the obsolete maxim of the Manchester economists, that labour is merely a sort of merchandise, of which the workman keeps a certain stock-in-trade, and that the capitalist's simple task, as a man of business, is to buy that labour as cheaply as possible, and that he has done with the seller as soon as his stock-in-trade is exhausted. Happily, a good many others understand now that in the long run this ridiculous theory is quite as bad for the State as killing was for the fowl which laid the golden eggs.

At all events, the feelings of the workman for his "patroon," as the old name still in use calls the employer, are none of the kindest. "Sweating" is a much less common occurrence in Holland than it was some twenty years ago, but while it would be mere demagogic clap-trap to speak of the remorseless exhaustion of labour by capital, there is nevertheless room enough for the cultivation of greater amenity between the two. And so it will remain for some time to come. Social legislation may do a great deal in the course of time, but it cannot do everything, and at best it must follow the awakening of the popular conscience. Hence progress must be made step by step, for nothing is so menacing to the stability of the social fabric as sudden changes, and a wise statesman prefers to let everyone of his acts do its own work, and produce its own consequences, before he risks the next move. The disintegration of social life is much worse than social misery, for disintegration makes misery universal, and throws innumerable obstacles in the way towards restoration.

And, however much the Dutch understand the

workman's feelings and position, however much they all long to see the latter improved, they also have learned enough of social and political history to know that for the community in general the only wise and safe principle of action is progress by degrees—evolution, not revolution.

CHAPTER VI

THE CANALS AND THEIR POPULATION

WHEN Drusus a few years before the commencement of our era excavated the Yssel canal, and thus gave a new arm to the Rhine, he began a process of canalisation in the Frisian and Batavian provinces which has been going on more or less ever since. To the foreigner Holland or the Northern Netherlands must always appear a land of dykes and canals, the one not more important for protection than the other as an artery of communication, spreading commerce and supporting national life. Napoleon, with naïve comprehensiveness, called Holland the alluvion of French rivers. Dutch patriots declare with legitimate pride, "God gave us the sea, but we made the shore," and no one who has seen the artificial barrier that guards the mainland from the Hook to the Texel, will disparage their achievement or scoff at their pretensions.

The sea-dyke saves Holland from the Northern Ocean, sombre and grey in its most genial mood, menacing and stormy for the long winter of our

Northern Hemisphere ; but it is to the inland dykes that protect the low-lying polders that Holland owes her prosperity and the sources of wealth which have made her inhabitants a nation. The original character of the country, a marshland intersected by the numerous channels of the Rhine and the Meuse, rendered it imperative that the system of dykes should be accompanied by a brother system of canals. The over-abundant waters had not merely to be arrested, they had to be confined and led off into prepared channels. In this manner also they were made to serve the purposes of man. Highroads across swamps were either impracticable or too costly; but canals furnished a sure and convenient means of transport and communication.

At the same time they did not imperil the security of the country. Roads on causeways or reared on sunken piles would have opened the door to an invader, but the canals provided an additional weapon of defence, for the opening of the dykes sufficed to turn the country again into its primeval state of marshland. The occasion on which this measure alone saved Holland during the French invasion of 1670 is a well-known passage in history, and the hopes of the Dutch in resisting the attack of any powerful aggressor would centre in the same measure of defence, which is the submerging of the country, practically speaking, under the waters of the canals and rivers. There exists a popular belief that

The Canals and their Population

there is at Amsterdam one master key, a turn of which would let loose the waters over the land, but whether it is well founded or not no one except a very few officials can say.

Pending any unfortunate necessity for breaking through the dykes and letting loose the waters, it may be observed in passing that the effectual maintenance of the dykes is a constant anxiety, and entails strenuous exertions. They stand in need of repeated repairing, and it is computed that they are completely reconstructed in the course of every four or five years. A sum of nearly a million sterling is spent annually on the work. A large and specially trained staff of engineers are in unceasing harness, a numerous band of dyke-watchers are constantly on the lookout, and when they raise the shout, " Come out! come out!" not a man, woman, or child must hold back from the summons to strengthen the weak points through which threatens to pass the flood that would overwhelm the land. It is a constant struggle with nature, in which the victory rests with man. As the dyke is the bulwark of Dutch prosperity in peace, it might be converted into the ally of despairing patriotism in war.

There are marked differences among the canals. The two largest and best-known canals, the North Canal and the North Sea Canal, are passages to the ocean for the largest ships, and specially intended to benefit the trade of Amsterdam. The

North Canal was made in 1819-25, soon after the restoration of the House of Orange, with an outlet at Helder, near the mouth of the Texel. It has a breadth of between 40 and 50 yards, a length of 50 miles, and a depth of 20 feet, which was then thought ample. After forty years' use this canal was found inadequate from every point of view. It was accordingly decided to construct a new canal direct from Amsterdam to Ymuiden across the narrowest strip of Holland. Although the Y was utilised, the labour on this canal was immense, and occupied a period of eleven years, being finally thrown open to navigation in 1877. In length it is under 16 miles, but its average breadth is 100 yards, and the depth varies from 23 to 27 feet. Consequently the largest ships from America or the Indies can reach the wharves of Amsterdam as easily as if it were a port on the sea-coast. Leaving aside the sea-passages that have been canalised among the islands of Zeeland, the remaining canals are inland waterways serving as the principal highways of the country, giving one part of the country access to the other, and especially serving as approaches or lanes to the great rivers Meuse and Rhine.

The interesting canal population of Holland is, of course, to be found on these canals, which are traversed in unceasing flow from year's end to year's end by the *tjalks*, or national barges. On these boats, which more resemble a lugger than a barge, they navigate not only the canals of their

A SEA-GOING CANAL

The Canals and their Population 67

own country, but the Rhine up to Coblentz, and even above that place. It has been computed that Germany imports half its food-supply through Rotterdam, and much of this is borne to its destined markets on *tjalks*. The William Canal connects Bois-le-Duc with Limburg, and saves the great bend of the Meuse. The Yssel connects with the Drenthe, the Orange and the Reitdiep canals, which convey to the Rhine the produce of remote Groningen and Friesland. The Rhine represents the destination of the bulk of the permanent canal population of Holland, whose floating habitations furnish one of the most interesting sights to be met with on the waters of the country, but which represent one of the secret phases of the people's life, into which few tourists or visitors have the opportunity of peering.

The canal population of Holland is fixed on a moderate computation at 50,000 persons. For this number of persons the barge represents the only fixed home, and the year passes in ceaseless movement across the inland waters of the country or on the great German river, excepting for the brief interval when the canals are frozen over in the depth of winter. Even during these periods of enforced idleness the barge does not the less continue to be their home, for the simple reason that the canal population possesses no other. Their whole life for generations, the bringing up and education of the children, the years of toil from youth to old age, are passed on these barges, which, varying in size and still more in condition, are as closely identified with the name of home in their owners' minds as if they were built of brick and stone on firm land. The ambition of the youth who tugs at the rope is to possess a *tjalk* of his own, and he diligently looks out for the maiden whose dowry will assist him, with his own savings, to make the purchase. This he may hope to procure for five or six hundred gulden, if he will be content with one of limited dimensions, and somewhat marked by time. When a family comes he will want a larger and more commodious boat, but by that time the profits which his first *tjalk* will have earned as a carrier will go far towards buying a second.

The *tjalks* are all built in the same form and from a common model. They carry a mast and sail, although for the greater part of their journeys they are towed by their owners, or rather by the families, wife and children, of the owner. Mynheer, the barge-owner, is usually to be seen smoking his pipe and taking his ease near the tiller. Formerly it was otherwise, for the towing was done by dogs, under the personal direction of, and no doubt with some assistance from, the barge-owner himself, while his wife and children remained on the poop of the boat. But five and twenty years ago the authorities of Amsterdam issued a law prohibiting the employment of dogs in the work of towing, and gradually this law was generally adopted and enforced throughout the country. When dogs were emancipated from their servitude on the canal-bank the family had to take their places, and by degrees the ease-loving head of the family has grown content to look on and think towing a labour reflecting on his dignity. There is nothing unusual in the sight of a barge being towed by an old woman, her daughter or daughter-in-law, and several children. As they strain at the rope the work seems extremely hard, but the people themselves appear unconscious of any hardship or inequality in the distribution of labour.

The barge is in the first place a conveyance. The whole of the front part of the boat represents the hold in which the cargo is placed. This is generally represented by cheese or vegetables, timber, peat, and stones, the last-named being a return-cargo for the repairing of dykes and the construction of quays. But in the second place it is a house or place of residence, and the stern of the boat is given up for that purpose. The living room is the raised deck or poop, on which is not only the tiller, but the cooking-stove. The sleeping-room forms the one covered-in apartment. It is easily divisible into two by a temporary or removable partition, and it always possesses the two little windows, one on each side of the tiller, which give it so great a resemblance to a doll's house. This resemblance is certainly heightened by the custom of colouring the barges, which are always painted a bright colour, red or green being perhaps the most usual. As ornament there is usually a good deal of brasswork; the handle of the tiller is generally bordered with the metal, and the owner seems to take pride in nailing brass along the bulwarks of his boat where it is not wanted and is even little seen. It has been suggested that the polishing of these brass plates or bars provides a pleasant change from the dull routine work of towing. The brightness of the paint and the brasswork constitutes the pride of the barge-owners, and supplies a standard of comparison among them.

To increase the homelike aspect of this water residence, birds and plants, always in greater or less quantity and variety, are to be seen either in the windows or on the deck. The poorest bargee, which generally means the youngest or the beginner, will have one song-bird in a gilt cage, and as he accumulates money in his really profitable calling, he will add to his collection of birds a row of flowers and bulbs in pots. Thus he says, with a glow of satisfaction, " I possess an aviary and a garden, like my cousin Hans on the polders, although my home is on the moving waters." To strengthen the illusion what does he do but fix a toy gate on the poop above his sleeping-cabin, and thus cherishes the belief that he is on his own domain. In the evening, when the towing is over for the day, the women bring out their sewing, the children play around the tiller, and the good man smokes his immense pipe with complete and indolent satisfaction. And so day passes on to day without a variation, and life runs by without a ripple or a murmur for the canal population, while the mere landsmen look on with envy at what seems to them an idyllic existence, and even ladies of breeding and high station have been known to declare that they would gladly change places with the mistress of the bargee's quarter-deck. That was no doubt in the days before women had to take on themselves the brunt and burden of the towing.

But even for the canal population of Holland the halcyon days are past. The spirit of reform is in the air. It may not be long before the *tjalk*, with its doll's house and its residential population, will finally disappear, and leave the canals of Holland as dull and colourless as the inland waters of any other country. The reform seems likely to come about in this way: There are at least 30,000 children resident on the canal-boats. How are they to be properly educated and brought up as useful citizens if they are to continue to lead a migratory existence, which never leaves them for a fortnight in a single place? Formerly nobody cared whether they were educated or not. They were left undisturbed to live their lives in their own simple and primitive way. As De Amicis wrote: " The children are born and grow up on the water; the boat carries all their small belongings, their domestic affections, their past, their present, and their future. They labour and save, and after many years they buy a larger boat, selling the old one to a family poorer than themselves, or handing it over to the eldest son, who in his turn installs his wife, taken from another boat, and seen for the first time in a chance meeting on the canal." But now the State has begun to interest itself in the children, and its intervention threatens to put a rude and summary ending to the system of heredity and exclusion which has kept the canal population a class apart.

For some time past schools have been in existence, especially devoted to the education of the barge children, and whenever the barges are moored in harbour the children are expected to attend them. But these periods of halting are very brief and uncertain. The stationary barge earns no money, and it may even be that the parents evade the law as far as possible for fear of seeing their children acquire a distaste for the life in which they have been brought up. But the Government, having taken one step in the matter, cannot afford to go back, and it must also have definite, satisfactory results to show for its legislation. The tentative measure of temporary schools along the canals has not leavened the illiteracy of the canal population. It will, therefore, become necessary at no great interval to devise some fresh and drastic regulations. Compulsory attendance at school for nine months of the year, which now applies to children in normal circumstances, may not be the lot of the barge children for some time, but when it comes, as it inevitably will some day, it will of necessity mean the break-up of the home life on the canals, for the children will have to be left behind during the almost unceasing voyages, and a place of residence will have to be provided on land. Where the children are the women will soon be, and gradually this place of residence will become the home, displacing the barge in the associations and affections of the canal population. Whether these changes will benefit those most affected by them cannot be guaranteed, but at least they will put an end to the separate existence of the canal population.

When this result has been compassed by the inexorable progress of education and knowledge, the gradual disappearance of the canal population, the class of hereditary bargees as we have known it, and as it still exists, may be expected to follow at no remote date, for it was based on the enforcement of the family principle, and on the devotion of a whole community, from its youngest to its eldest member, to its maintenance. As it is, the tow-barge is something of an anachronism, but the withdrawal of the youthful recruits, whose up-bringing alone rendered it possible, will entail its inevitable extinction. The decay and break-up of the guild of *tjalk* owners will be hastened by the introduction of steam and electricity as means of locomotion. The canals will lose the bright-coloured barges which are to-day their most striking feature, and the population that has so long floated over their surface. Life will be duller and more monotonous. The canal population, so long distinct, will be merged in the rest of the community. The tug will displace the tow-rope. The pullers will be housed on land, mastering the three R's instead of learning to strain at the girth.

But there is still a brief period left during which the canal population may be seen in its original primitive existence, devoted to the barge, which is the only home known to six or seven thousand families, and traversing the water roads of their country in unceasing and endless progression. There is nothing like it in any other country of Europe. Venice has its water routes, but the gondola is not a domicile. There was a canal population in England, but, like much else in our modern life, it has lost whatever picturesqueness it might once have claimed. For a true canal population, bright and happy, living the same life from father to son and generation to generation, we must go to Holland. There these inland navigators ply their vocation with only one ambition, and that to become the owner of a *tjalk*, and to rear thereon a family of towers. It is said that the life is one that requires the consumption of unlimited quantities of *schnapps* and the humidity of the atmosphere is undoubted. But even free libations do not diminish the prosperity of the bargees. They are a thriving race, and it must also be noted to their credit that they are well behaved, and not given to quarrels. Collisions on the thickly-covered canals are rare; malicious collisions are unknown. The barges pass and repass without hindrance, the tow-ropes never get entangled, there is mutual forbearance, and the skill derived from long experience in slipping the ropes under the barges does the rest. The conditions under which the canal population exists and thrives are a survival of an older order of things. When they disappear another of the few picturesque heritages of mediæval life will have been removed from the hurly-burly and fierce competition of modern existence.

CHAPTER VII

A DUTCH VILLAGE

VILLAGES in Holland are towns in miniature, for the simple reason that when you have a marsh to live in you drain a part of it and build on that part, and so build in streets, and do not form a village as in England, by houses dotted here and there round a green or down leafy lanes. The village green in Holland is the village street or square in front of the church or *Raadhuis*. Here the children play, for you cannot play in a swamp, and that is what polder land is seven months out of the year, and so we find that a Dutch village in most parts of the country is a town in miniature. Thirty years ago the *Raadhuis* would have been the village inn, barber's shop, and the principal hotel all rolled into one, and the innkeeper, as a natural consequence, the wealthiest man in the neighbourhood. The farmers would have sat at the *Raad, i. e.*, the Village Council, with their caps over their eyes, long Gouda pipes in their mouths, and a *glaasje klare* (*Schiedam*) under their chairs which they would have steadily sipped at intervals, puffing at their pipes during the whole sitting. Their wooden shoes (*klompen*), scrubbed for the occasion to a brilliant white with the help of a good layer of whitening, might have been seen in a row standing on the door-mat, for no well-educated farmer would ever have dreamed of entering a room with shoes on his feet, and he would have taken his *pruim* or quid of tobacco, which every farmer chews even when smoking, out of his mouth and laid it on the window-sill, the usual receptacle for such things, and there it would lie in its own little circle of brown fluid to be replaced either in his own or his neighbour's mouth after the meeting was over. Nowadays a farmer goes to the *Raad* dressed in a suit of black clothes and with his feet encased in leather boots. He never wears *klompen* save when at work in the field or on the farm. He also talks of his *Gemeente* for all Holland is portioned off into *Gemeenten* and a village is such in as good a sense as large towns like The Hague and Amsterdam, and better, if anything, for the taxes there are not so high. Each *Gemeente* is separately governed by a Burgomaster and *Leden van den Raad*, which is nothing more nor less than a County Council, presided over by a prominent man nominated by the sovereign, and not elected by the members, of which some are called *Wethouders*, and are, like the other members, elected by the residents of the district. These *Wethouders*, with the Burgomaster, form the *Dagelyksch Bestuur*. All ordinary matters concerning the *Gemeente*, such as giving information to the Minister of War about the men who have signed for the militia, or about any person living in their *Gemeenten* are regulated by the *Dagelyksch Bestuur*, though matters of import are brought before the *Raad*. Next in importance to the Burgomaster come the *Gemeente-ontvanger*, who receives all the taxes, and the "Notary," who is the busiest man in the village, although the doctor and clergyman or priest have a large share in the work of contributing to the welfare of the villagers.

A village clergyman is an important person, for he is held in high honour by his parishioners, and his larder is always well stocked free of cost. His income, also, is relatively larger than that of a town pastor, for, besides his fixed salary, he reaps a nice little revenue from the pastures belonging to the *pastorij*, which he lets out to farmers. The schoolmaster, on the contrary, is treated with but little consideration, and he often feels decidedly like a fish out of water, for, though belonging by birth to the labouring class, he is too well educated to associate with his former companions and yet not sufficiently refined to move in the village "society," besides which he would not be able to return hospitality, as his salary only amounts to from £40 to £60 a year, and nowhere is the principle of reciprocity more observed than in Dutch hospitality in certain

A Dutch Village

classes. In very small villages many offices are combined in one person, and so we find a prominent inhabitant blacksmith, painter, and carpenter, while the baker's shop is a kind of universal provider for the villagers' simple wants. The butcher is the only person who is the man of one occupation, though he, too, goes round to the neighbouring farms to help in the slaughtering of the cattle, and sometimes lends a hand in the salting and storing of the meat.

The farmers live just outside the village, and only come there when they go to the *Raad* or on Saturday evenings when the week's work is done. They then visit the barber before meeting at the *café* for their weekly game of billiards. Every resident of the village also betakes himself to his "club" or *Societeit* on Saturday night, and just as the *Mindere man, i. e.,* farmers and labourers, have their games and discuss their farms, their cattle, and the price of hay or corn, so, too, the *Notabelen* discuss every subject under the sun, not forgetting their dear neighbours.

On Sunday mornings the whole *Gemeente* goes to church, from the Burgomaster to the poorest farm-labourer, and all are dressed in their best. The men of the village have put aside their working-clothes, and are attired in blue or black cloth suits, with white shirt fronts and coloured ties. The women have donned black dresses, caps, and shawls, and carry their scent-bottles, peppermints, and *gezangboek* (hymnbook) with large golden clasps. The *Stovenzetster*, a woman who acts as verger, shows the good people to their seats and provides the women, if the weather is cold, with *warme stoven* (hot stoves), to keep their feet comfortable. These little "stoves" contain little three-cornered green or brown pots (*testen*), in which pieces of glowing peat are put, and sometimes when the peat is not quite red-hot it smokes terribly, and gives a most unpleasant odour to the building. The women survive it, however, by resorting to their *eau de Cologne*, which they sprinkle upon their handkerchiefs, and keep passing to their neighbours during the whole service.

The village schoolmaster has a special office to perform in the Sunday service. It is he who reads a chapter to them before the entrance of the clergyman, who comes only when service has begun. Then the sermon, which is the chief part of the service in Dutch churches, begins. This sermon is very long, and the congregation sleep through the first part very peacefully, but the rest is not for long, for when the "domine" has spoken for about three-quarters of an hour he calls upon his congregation to sing a verse of some particular psalm. The schoolmaster starts the singing, which goes very slowly, each note lasting at least four beats, so that the tune is completely lost. However, as a rule, everyone

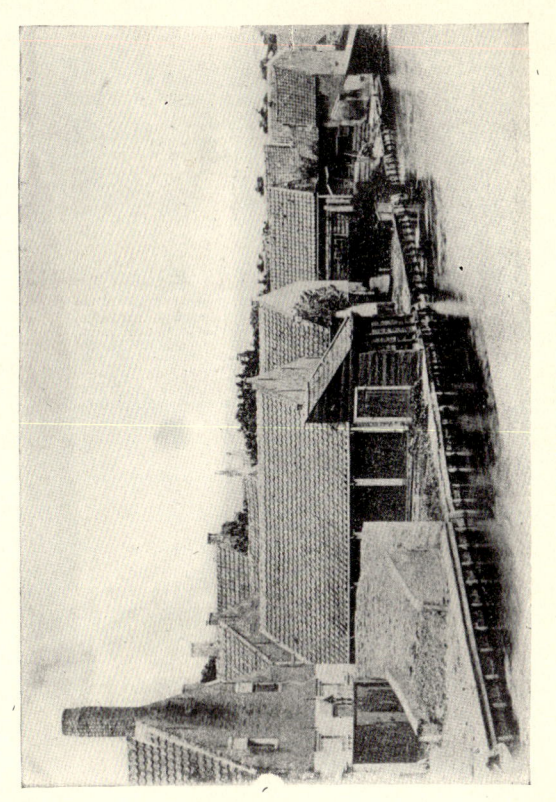

A VILLAGE IN DYKE-LAND

tenant are in some respects still feudalistic, and hence very old-fashioned. On some estates the landlord has still the right of exacting personal service from his tenants, and can call upon them to come and plough his field with their horses, or help with the harvesting, for which service they are paid one " gulden," or 1s. 8d. a day, which, of course, is not the full value of their labour. The tenants likewise ask their landlord's consent to their marriages, and it is refused if the man or woman is not considered suitable or respectable.

A farmer who keeps two or three cows pays a rent of £8 a year for his farm, which only yields enough to keep him and his family—not in a high standard of living either. The rent is generally calculated at the rate of three per cent. of the value. He pays his farm-labourers 80 cents, or 1s. 4d., for a day's work. In former days, however, money was never given, and the wages of a farm-servant then were a suit of clothes, a pair of boots, and some linen, while the women received an apron, some linen, and a few petticoats once a year. Now they get, in addition to this, £12 a year. In Gramsbergen (Overyssel) a whole family, consisting of a mother, her daughter and her two grown-up sons, earned no more than four or five guilders (8s. or 10s.) between them, but then they lived rent free. It is not wonderful, therefore, that farm-labourers are scarce, and that many a young man, unable to earn enough to keep body and soul together decently, seeks work in the factories here or in Belgium,[1] while those who do not wish to give up agricultural pursuits migrate to Germany, where the demand for "hands" is greater and the wages consequently higher. In former days strangers came to this country to earn money. Now the tables are turned, and the fact that Holland is situated between two countries whose thriving industries demand a greater number of workers every year will yet bring serious trouble and loss to Dutch agriculture.[2]

[1] According to a recent return, 56,506 Netherlands workmen are employed in Belgium.

[2] Just now great results are expected from the "allotment system," of which a trial has been made in Friesland on the extensive possessions of Mr. Jansen, of Amsterdam.

CHAPTER IX

RURAL CUSTOMS

THE Hollander is a very conservative individual, and therefore some curious customs still prevail among the peasant and working classes in the Netherlands, especially in the Eastern Provinces, for there the people are most primitive, and there it is that we find many queer old rhymes, apparently without any sense in them, but which must have had their origin in forgotten national or domestic events. A remnant of an old pagan custom of welcoming the summer is still to be seen in many country places. On the Saturday before Whitsunday, very early in the morning, a party of children may be seen setting out towards the woods to gather green boughs. After dipping these in water they return home in triumph and place them before the doors of those who were not " up with the lark " in such a manner that when these long sleepers open them, the wet green boughs will come tumbling down upon their heads. Very often, too, the children pursue the late risers, and beat them with the branches, jeering at them the while, and singing about the laziness of the sluggard. These old songs have undergone very many variations, and nowadays one cannot say which is the correct and original form. They have, in fact, been hopelessly mixed up with other songs, and in no two provinces do we find exactly the same versions. The *luilakfeest*,[1] of which I have just spoken, goes by the name of *Dauwtrappen* ("treading the dew") in some parts of the country, but the observance of it is the same wherever the custom obtains.

Eiertikken at Easter must also not be overlooked. For a whole week before Easter the peasant children go round from house to house begging for eggs, and carrying a wreath of green leaves stuck on a long stick. This stick and wreath they call their *Palm Paschen* which really means Palm Sunday, and may have been so called because they make the wreath on that day.

Down the village streets they go, singing all the while and waving the wreath above their heads:

> " Palm, Palm Paschen,
> Hei koeerei.
> Weldra is het Paschen,
> Dan hebben wy een ei.
> Een ei—twee ei,
> Het derde is het Paschei."

[1] This day is called *Luilak* (sluggard) in some parts of the country and the feast is called *Luilakfeest*.

PALM PASCHEN—BEGGING FOR EGGS

Rural Customs 101

["Palm, Palm Sunday,
  Hei koeerei.
  Soon it will be Easter,
  And we shall have an egg.
  One egg—two eggs,
  The third egg is the Easter egg."]

They knock at every farmhouse, and are very seldom sent away empty-handed. When they have collected enough eggs to suit their purpose — generally three or four apiece — they boil them hard and stain them with two different colours, either brown with coffee or red with beet-root juice, and then on Easter Day they all repair to the meadows carrying their eggs with them, and the *eiertikken* begins. The children sit down on the grass and each child knocks one of his eggs against that of another in such a way that only one of the shells breaks. The child whose egg does not break wins, and becomes the possessor of the broken egg.

The strangest of all these begging-customs, however, is the one in vogue between Christmas and Twelfth Night. Then the children go out in couples, each boy carrying an earthenware pot, over which a bladder is stretched, with a piece of stick tied in the middle. When this stick is twirled about, a not very melodious grumbling sound proceeds from the contrivance, which is known by the name of *rommelpot*. By going about in this manner the children are able to collect some few pence to buy bread—or gin—

for their fathers. When they stop before anyone's house, they drawl out: " Give me a cent, and I will pass on, for I have no money to buy bread." The origin both of the custom and song is shrouded in mystery.[1]

Besides the customs in vogue at such festive seasons as Whitsuntide, Easter, and Christmas, there are yet others of more everyday occurrence which are well worth the knowing. In Overyssel, for instance, we find a very sensible one indeed. It is usual there, when a family moves to another part of the village, or when they settle elsewhere, for the people living in the neighbourhood to bring them presents to help furnish their new house. Sometimes these presents include poultry or even a pig, which, though they do not so much furnish the house as the table, prove nevertheless very acceptable. As soon as all the moving is over and they are comfortably installed in their new home, the next thing to do is to invite all the neighbours to a party.

This is a very important social duty and ought on no account to be omitted, as it entitles host and hostess to the help of all their guests in the event of illness or adversity taking place in their family. If, however, they do not conform to this

[1] A Society of Research into old folk-lore and folk-song has recently been founded by some of the leading Dutch literary authorities, who also propose to publish a little periodical in which all these customs will be collected and noted.

social obligation, their neighbours and friends stand aloof and do not so much as move a finger to help them. Should one of the family fall ill, the four nearest male neighbours are called in. These men fetch the doctor, and do all the nursing. They will even watch by the invalid at night, and so long as the illness lasts they undertake all the farm-work. Sometimes they will go on working the farm for years, and when a widow is left with young children in straitened circumstances, these *noodburen* (neighbours in need) will help her in all possible ways and take all the business and worry off her hands.

In case of a marriage, too, the neighbours do the greater part of the preparations. They invite the relations and friends to come to the wedding, and make ready the feast. The invitations are always given by word of mouth, and two young men [1] closely related to the bride and bridegroom are appointed to go round from house to house to bid the people come. They are dressed for this purpose in their best Sunday clothes, and wear artificial flowers and six peacock's feathers in their caps. The invitation is made in poetry, in which the assurance is conveyed that there will be plenty to eat and plenty of gin and beer to drink, and that whatever they may have omitted to say will be told by the bride and bridegroom

[1] In Gelderland we find this same custom and also in Friesland, but in this last-named province the invitation is given by two young girls.

at the feast. This verse in the native patois is very curious:

"GOËN DAG!

"Daor stao'k op minen staf,
  En weet niet wat ik zeggen mag;
Nou hek me weer bedacht
  En weet ik wat ik zeggen mag:
Hier stürt ons Gart van Vente als brügom
En Mientje Elschot as de brüd,
  Ende' nöget uwder üt
  Margen vrog om tien ür
Op en tonne bier tiene twalevenne,
  Op en anker wîn, vif, zesse
En en wanne vol rozinen.
  De' zült by Venterboer verschinen
  Met de hüsgezeten
  En nüms vergeten,
Vrog kommen en late bliven
  Anders kün wy 't nie 't op krigen.
Lüstig ezongen, vrolik esprongen,
  Springen met de deide beene,
  En wat ik nog hebbe vergeten
Zult ow de brügom ende brüd verbeten.
Hej my elk nuw wal verstaan
  Dan laot de fles üm de taofel gaon."

"GOOD DAY!

[" I rest here on my stick,
  I don't know what to say;
Now I have thought of it
  And know what I may say:
Here sent us Gart van Vente, the bridegroom,
And Mientje Elschot, the bride,
  To invite you

Rural Customs 105

> To-morrow morning at ten o'clock
> To empty ten or twelve barrels of beer,
> Five or six hogsheads of wine,
> And a basket full of dried grapes.
> You will come to the house of Venterboer
> With all your inmates
> And forget nobody.
> Come early and remain late,
> Else we can't swallow it all down.
> Then sing cheerfully, leap joyfully,
> Leap with both your legs.
> And, what I have yet forgotten,
> Think of the bridegroom and bride.
> If you have understood me well
> Let pass the bottle round the table."]

The day before the wedding is to take place the bridegroom and some of his friends arrive at the bride's house in a cart, drawn by four horses, to bring away the bride and her belongings. These latter are a motley collection, for they consist not only of her clothes, bed, and bed-curtains, but her spinning-wheel, linen-press full of linen, and also a cow. After everything has been loaded upon the cart, and the young men have refreshed themselves with *rystebrij* (rice boiled with sweet milk), they drive away in state, singing as they go. The following day the bride is married from the house of her parents-in-law, and, as it often happens that the young couple live with the bridegroom's people, it is only natural that they like to have the house in proper order before the arrival of the wedding-guests, who begin to appear as soon as eight o'clock in the morning. When all the invited guests are assembled and have partaken of hot gin mixed with currants, handed round in two-handled pewter cups, kept especially for these occasions, the whole party goes about eleven o'clock to the *Stadhuis*, or Town Hall, where the couple are married before the Burgomaster, and afterwards to the church, where the blessing is given upon their union. On returning home the mid-day meal is ready, which, on this festive occasion, consists of ham, potatoes, and salt fish, and the clergyman is also honoured with an invitation to the gathering. The rest of the day is spent in rejoicings, in which eating and drinking take the chief part. The bride changes her outer apparel about four times during the day, always in public, standing before her linen-press. The day is wound up with a dance, for which the village fiddler provides the music, the bride opening the ball with one of the young men who invited the guests, and she then presents him with a fine linen handkerchief as a reward for his invaluable services on the occasion.

In Friesland a curious old custom still exists, called the *Joen-piezl*, which furnishes the clue to an odd incident in Mrs. Schreiner's *Story of an African Farm*. When a man and girl are about to be married, they must first sit up for a whole night in the kitchen with a burning candle on the table between them. By the time the candle is burnt low in its socket, they must have found out whether they really are fond of each other.

The marriage customs in North and South Holland are very different to the former. As soon as a couple are *aangeteekend*, *i. e.*, when the banns are published for the first time (which does not happen in church, but takes the form of a notice put up at the Town Hall), and have returned from the *Stadhuis*, they drive about and take a bag of sweets (*bruidsuikers*) to all their friends. On the wedding-day, after the ceremony is over, the bride and bridegroom again drive out together in a " chaise "—a high carriage on very big wheels, with room for but two persons. The horse's head, the whip, and the reins are all decorated with flowers and coloured ribbons. The wedding-guests drive in couples behind the bride and bridegroom's " chaise," and the progress is called *Speuleryden*. Sometimes they drive for miles across country, stopping at every *café* to drink brandy and sugar, and when they pass children on the road these call out to them: *Bruid, bruid, strooi je suikers uit* (" Bride, bride, strew your sugars about "). Handfuls of sweets will thereupon be seen flying through the air and rolling about the ground, while the children tumble over each other in their eager haste to collect as many of these sweets as they can. Sometimes as much as twenty-five pounds of sweets are thus scattered upon the roadside for the village children. Such a wedding is quite an event in the lives of these little ones, and they will talk for weeks to come about the amount of sweets they were able to procure.

At Ryswyk, a little village near The Hague, and in most villages in Westland, South Holland, the bride and bridegroom present to the Burgomaster and *Wethouders*, and also to the *Ambtenaar van den Burgerlyken Stand*, who marries them at the *Stadhuis*, a bag of these sweets, while one bearing the inscription, "Compliments of bride and bridegroom," is given to the officiating clergyman immediately after the ceremony in church. On their way home all along the road they strew *suikers* out of the carriage windows for the gaping crowds. Some of the less well-to-do farmers, and those who live near large towns, give their wedding-parties at a *café* or *uitspanning*. This word means literally a place where the horse is taken out of the shafts, but it is also a restaurant with a garden attached to it, in which there are swings and seesaws, upon which the guests disport themselves during the afternoon, while in the evening a large hall in the building is arranged for the ball, for that is the conclusion of every *boeren-bruiloft*. Very often the ball lasts till the cock-crowing, and then, if the *Bruiloft-houers* are Roman Catholics, it is no uncommon practice first to go to church and "count their beads" before they disperse on their separate ways to begin the duties of a new day.

Rural Customs

A birth is naturally an occasion that calls for very festive celebration. When the child is about a week old, its parents send round to all their friends to come and rejoice with them. The men are invited *op een lange pyp en een bitterje*, the women for the afternoon *op suikerdebol*. At twelve o'clock the men begin to arrive, and are immediately provided with a long Gouda pipe, a pouch of tobacco, and a cut-glass bottle containing gin mixed with aromatic bitters. While they smoke, they talk in voices loud enough to make anyone who is not acquainted with a farmer's mode of speech think that a great deal of quarrelling is going on in the house. This entertainment lasts till seven o'clock, when all the men leave and the room is cleared, though not ventilated, and the table is rearranged for the evening's rejoicings.

Dishes of bread and butter, flat buttered rusks liberally spread with *muisjes* (sugared aniseed—the literal translation is " mice "), together with tarts and sweets of all descriptions, are put out in endless profusion on all the best china the good wife possesses. For each of the guests two of these round flat rusks are provided, two being the correct number to take, for more than two would be considered greedy, and to eat only one would be sure to offend the hostess. Eating and drinking, for *Advocate borrel* (brandy and eggs) is also served, go on for the greater part of the afternoon. The midday meal is altogether dispensed with on such a day, and, judging by appearances, one cannot say that the guests look as if they had missed it!

It is quite the national custom to eat rusks with *muisjes* on these occasions, and these little sweets are manufactured of two kinds. The sugar coating is smooth when the child is a girl, and rough and prickly like a chestnut burr when the child is a boy; and when one goes to buy *muisjes* at a confectioner's he is always asked whether boys' or girls' *muisjes* are required. Hundreds-and-thousands, the well-known decoration on buns and cakes in an English pastrycook's shop, bear the closest resemblance to these Dutch *muisjes*.

When a little child is born into a family of the better classes, the servants are treated to biscuits and "mice" on that day; while in the very old-fashioned Dutch families there is still another custom, that of offering *Kandeel*, a preparation of eggs and Rhine wine or hock, on the first day the young mother receives visitors, and it is specially made for these occasions by the *baker* (nurse).

Funeral processions are a very mournful sight on all occasions, but a Dutch funeral depresses one for about a month after. The hearse is all hung with black draperies, while on the box sits the coachman wearing a large black hat called *huilebalk*. From the rim overlapping the face hangs a piece of black cord. This he holds

KERMIS—"HOS-EN-HOSSEN—HI-HA"
AFTER THE PICTURE BY VAN GELDROP

in his mouth to prevent the hat from falling off his head. The hearse itself is generally embellished by the images of grinning skulls, though the carriages following the hearse have no distinctive mark. If such a funeral procession happens to come along the road you yourself are going, you may be sure of enjoying its company the whole way, for the horses are only allowed to walk, never trot, and it takes hours to get to the cemetery. In former days the horses were specially shod for this occasion in such a way that they went lame on one leg. This end was achieved by driving the nail of the shoe into the animal's foot, for people thought this added to the doleful aspect of the *cortége* as it advanced slowly along the road. Happily, this cruelty is now dispensed with, and indeed is entirely forbidden by the Society for the Prevention of Cruelty to Animals, but the ugly aspect of the hearses remains the same.

At a death, the relatives of the deceased have large cards printed, announcing the family loss. These cards are taken round to every house in the neighbourhood by a man specially hired for the purpose. This man, called an *aanspreker* carries a list of the names and addresses of the people on whom he has to leave cards; if the people sending out the cards have friends in any other street of the town, a card is left at every house in that street.

If the deceased was an officer, the cards, besides

being sent round in the neighbourhood, are left at every officer's house throughout the town. To whichever profession the deceased belonged, to the people of that profession the cards are sent. A Minister of State or any other person occupying a very high position sends cards to every house in the town and suburbs.

In a village or country place a funeral is rather a popular event, and the preparations for it somewhat resemble the preparations for a feast. This, for instance, is the case in Overyssel. When one of a family dies, the nearest relatives immediately call in the neighbouring women, and these take upon themselves all the necessary arrangements. They send round messages announcing the death and day of interment; they buy coffee, sugar-candy, and a bottle of gin, wherewith to refresh themselves while making the shroud and dressing the dead body; and the next morning they take care that the church bells are duly rung, and, in the afternoon, when the relations and friends come to offer their condolences, they serve them, as they sit round the bier, with black bread and coffee. When the plates and cups are empty the visitors leave again without having spoken a word.

On the day of the funeral, the guests assemble at two o'clock in the afternoon. They first sit round the tables and eat and drink in silence, and when the first batch have satisfied their appetites they move away and make room for

Rural Customs

others. After this meal all walk round the coffin, and repeat one after another, "*'T was een goed mensch*" ("He" or "she was a good man or woman," as the case may be). Then the lid of the coffin is fastened down with twelve wooden pegs, which the most honoured guest is allowed to hammer in, and the coffin is forthwith placed on an ordinary farm-cart. The nearest relations get in, too, and sit on the coffin, and the other women on the cart facing the coffin. This custom is adhered to, notwithstanding the prohibition by law to sit on any conveyance carrying a coffin. The women are in mourning from tip to toe, and closely enveloped in black merino shawls, which they wear over their heads. The men follow on foot, and it is a picturesque though melancholy sight to watch these funeral processions, always at close of day, solemnly wending their way along the road, the dark figures of the women silhouetted against a sky all aglow with those glorious sunsets for which Overyssel is famous.

CHAPTER X

KERMIS AND ST. NICHOLAS

OF all the festivals and occasions of popular rejoicing and merriment in Holland, none can compare with the Kermis and the Festival of St. Nicholas, which are in many ways peculiarly characteristic of Dutch life and Dutch love for primitive usage. The Kermis is particularly popular, because of the manifold amusements which are associated with it, and because it unites all classes of the population in the common pursuit of unsophisticated pleasure. As its name implies, the Kermis (*Kerk-mis*) has a religious origin, being named after the chief part of the Church service, the mass. Just as the Feast of St. Baro received the name *Bamisse*, so that of the consecration of the church was called the "Church-mass," or *Kerk-mis*. In ancient times, if a church was consecrated on the name-day of a certain saint the church was also dedicated to that saint. Such a festival was a chief festival, or *Hoofd-feest*, for a church, and it was not only celebrated with great pomp and solemnity, but amusements of all kinds were

Kermis and St. Nicholas

added to give the celebration a more festive character. In large towns there were Kermissen at different times of the year in different parishes, for each church was dedicated to a different saint, so that there were as many dedicatory feasts in a town as there were churches in it.

At a very early period in the nation's history the Church-masses began to wear a more worldly character, for the merchants made them an occasion for introducing their wares and trading with the people, just as they did at the ordinary "year-markets." These year-markets always fell on the same day as the Kermissen, but they had a different origin. They were held by permission of the Sovereign, and were first instituted to encourage trade; but gradually the Kermis and the year-market went hand-in-hand, for the people could no longer imagine a year-market without the Kermis amusements, or a Kermis without booths and stalls, so if there was not sufficient room for the latter to be built on the streets or squares, the priest allowed them to be put up in the churchyard or sometimes even in the church. Moreover, if it was not possible to have the year-market in the same week as the Kermis, then the Kermis was put off to suit the year-market, and these latter were of great aid to the religious festivals, for they attracted a greater number of people, and as dispensations were given for attending the masses both the churches and the markets were benefited. The mass lasted eight days, and the year-market as long as the Church festival. The Church protected the year-markets, and rang them in. With the first stroke of the Kermis clock, the year-market was opened and the first dance commenced, followed by a grand procession, in which all the principal people of the town took part, and when the last stroke died away white crosses were nailed upon all the bridges, and on the gates of the town. These served both as a passport and also as a token of the *markt vrede* (market peace), so that anyone seeing the cross knew that he might enter the town and buy and sell *ad libitum*, also that his peace and safety were guaranteed, and that anyone who disturbed the *markt vrede* would be banished from the place, and not be allowed to come back another year. In some places this yearly market was named, after the crosses, *Cruyce-markt*.

Very festive is the appearance of a town in the Kermis week. On the opening day at twelve o'clock the bells of the cathedral or chief church are set ringing, and this is the sign for the booths to be opened and the *Kermispret* to begin. Everywhere tempting stores are displayed to view, and although a scent of oil and burning fat pervades the air, nobody seems to mind that, for it only increases the delight the Kermis has in store for them. The stalls are generally set out in two rows. The most primitive of these is the stall of hard-boiled eggs and pickled gherkins, whose owner is probably a Jew, and pleasant sounds his hoarse voice while praising his wares high above all others. If he does prevail upon you to come and try one of his eggs and gherkins it only adds more relish to your meal when he tells you of the man who only paid one cent for a large gherkin which really cost two, and although he already had put it in his mouth he made him put the other part back. Or when you go to eat *poffertjes*, which look so tempting, and with the first bite find a quid of tobacco in the inoffensive-looking little morsel, do not let this trifling incident disturb your equanimity, but try another booth. It is quite worth your while to stand in front of a *poffertjeskraam* and see how they are made. The batter is simply buckwheat-meal mixed with water, and some yeast to make it light. Over a bright fire of logs is placed a large, square, iron baking-sheet with deep impressions for the reception of the batter. On one side sits a woman on a high stool, with a bowl of the mixture by her side and a large wooden ladle in her hand. This she dips into the batter, bringing it out full, then with a quick sweep of the arm she empties its contents into the hollows of the baking sheet. A man standing by turns them dexterously one by one with a steel fork, and a moment later he pricks them six at a time on to the fork ; this he does four times to get a plateful, and then he hands it over to another man inside the booth, who adds a pat of butter and a liberal sprinkling of sugar. The *wafelkramen* are not so largely patronised, as the price of these delicacies is rather too high for the slender purses of the average *Kermis houwer*, but *oliebollen*—round, ball-shaped cakes swimming in oil—are within the reach of all, as they cost but a cent apiece. Servants and their lovers, after satisfying their appetites with these *oliebollen* go and have a few turns in the roundabouts by way of a change, and then hurry to the fish-stall, where they eat a raw salted herring to counteract the effects of the earlier dissipation. The more respectable servant, however, turns up her nose at the herrings, and goes in for smoked eel. These fish-stalls are very quaint in appearance, for they are hung with garlands of dried *scharretje* (a white, thin, leathery-looking fish), which dangle in front, and form a most original decoration. In the towns a separate day and evening are set apart for the servant classes to go to the fair, and there is also a day for the *élite*.

At the commencement of the reign of King William III. the whole Court, including the King and Queen, used to meet at The Hague Kermis on the Lange Voorhout on Thursday afternoons between two and four o'clock, and walk up and down between the double row of stalls; and in the evening of that day they all visited either the most renowned circus of the season or went to see the *Kermis stuk*, or special play acted in fair-time.

Kermis and St. Nicholas

The servants' evening, as it is held in Rotterdam, is the most characteristic. It is an evening shunned by the more respectable people, for the *Kermisgangers* are a very rowdy lot. They amuse themselves chiefly by running along the streets in long rows, arm-in-arm, singing *Hossen — hossen — hossen!* They also treat each other to *Nieuw rood met suiker* — black currants preserved in gin with sugar—until they are all quite tipsy, and woe to any quiet pedestrian who has the misfortune to pass their way, for with loud "Hi-ha's" they encircle him and make him *hos* with them. The evening is commonly called the *Aalbessen* (black-currant) *hos*.

An equally curious but not so bad a custom is the Groninger *Koek eten*. All Groningers are fond of cake, and the *Groninger kauke* is a widespread and very tasty production; but for this special purpose is used the *ellekoek*, a very long thin cake, which, as its name implies, is sold by the yard. It is very tough, and just thin enough to hold in a large mouth, and when a man chooses a girl to keep Kermis with him they must first see whether they will suit one another as *Vrijer* and *Vrijster* by eating *ellekoek*. This is done in the following manner. They stand opposite one another, and each begins at an end and eats towards the other. They may not touch the cake with their hands, but must hold it between their teeth all the while they are eating, and if they are unable to accomplish this feat and kiss when they get to the middle it is a sure sign that they are not suited to one another, and so the partnership is not concluded. In some parts of Friesland and in Voorburg, one of the many villages near The Hague, there is another cake custom, the *Koekslaan*, which is a sort of cake lottery. The cakes are all put out on large blocks, which are higher at the sides than in the middle, and for twopence anyone who likes may try his luck and see if he can break the cake in two by striking it with a stout stick provided by the stall-keeper for the purpose. It is necessary to do this in one blow, for a second try involves the payment of another fee. He who succeeds carries off the broken cake, and receives a second one as a prize. Some men are very clever at this, and manage to carry off a good many prizes.

Just as the Kermis is rung in by the bells, so also it is tolled out again. This, however, is not an official proceeding, but a custom among the schoolboys of the Gymnasium and Higher Burgher Schools. At The Hague on the last day of the fair all the *schooljeugd* used to assemble in the Lange Voorhout, dressed in black, just as they would dress for a funeral, while four of them carried a bier, hung with wreaths and black draperies. On this bier was supposed to rest all that remained of the Kermis. In front of the bier walked a boy ringing a large bell, and pro-

Kermis and St. Nicholas

claiming: *De Kermis is dood, de Kermis wordt begraven* ("The Kermis is dead, and is going to be buried"). Behind the bier came all the other boys with the most mournful expression upon their faces they could muster for the occasion, and thus they carried the "dead fair" through the principal streets of the town, and at last buried it in the Scheveningsche Boschjes. But this custom is now a thing of the past, for the Kermis at The Hague has been abolished, even as it has been abolished in most of the other towns throughout the kingdom, for all authorities were agreed that fair-time promoted vice and drunkenness, and the old-fashioned Kermis is now only to be found in Rotterdam, Leyden, Delft, and some of the smaller provincial towns and villages.

The 6th of December is the day dedicated to St. Nicholas, and its vigil is one of the most characteristic of Dutch festivals. It is an evening for family reunions, and is filled with old recollections for the elders and new delights for the younger people and children. Just as English people give presents at Christmas-time, so do the Dutch at St. Nicholas, only in a different way, for St. Nicholas presents must be hidden and disguised as much as possible, and be accompanied by rhymes explaining what the gift is and for whom St. Nicholas intends it. Sometimes a parcel addressed to one person will finally turn out to be for quite a different member of the family than the one who first received it, for the address on each wrapper in the various stages of unpacking makes it necessary for the parcel to change hands as many times as there are papers to undo. The tiniest things are sent in immense packing-cases, and sometimes the gifts are baked in a loaf of bread or hidden in a turf, and the longer it takes before the present is found the more successful is the "surprise."

The greatest delight to the giver of the parcel is to remain unknown as long as possible, and even if the present is sent from one member of the family to another living in the same house the door-bell is always rung by the servant before she brings the parcel in, to make believe that it has come from some outsider, and if a parcel has to be taken to a friend's house it is very often entrusted to a passer-by with the request to leave it at the door and ring the bell. In houses where there are many children, some of the elders dress up as the good Bishop St. Nicholas and his black servant. The children are always very much impressed by the knowledge St. Nicholas shows of all their shortcomings, for he usually reminds them of their little failings, and gives them each an appropriate lecture. Sometimes he makes them repeat a verse to him or asks them about their lessons, all of which tends to make the moment of his arrival looked forward to with much excitement and some trembling, for St. Nicholas generally announces at what time he is to be expected, so that all may be in readiness for his reception.

On the eventful evening a large white sheet is laid out upon the floor in the middle of the room, and round it stand all the children with sparkling eyes and flushed faces, eagerly scrutinising the hand of the clock. As soon as it points to five minutes before the expected time of the Saint's arrival they begin to sing songs to welcome him to their midst, and ask him to give as liberally as was his wont, meanwhile praising his goodness and greatness in the most eloquent terms. The first intimation the children get of the Saint's arrival is a shower of sweets bursting in upon them. Then, amid the general scramble which ensues, St. Nicholas suddenly makes his appearance in full episcopal vestments, laden with presents, while in the rear stands his black servant with an open sack in one hand in which to put all the naughty boys and girls, and a rod in the other which he shakes vigorously from time to time. When the presents have all been distributed, and St. Nicholas has made his adieus, promising to come back the following year, and the children are packed to bed to dream of all the fun they have had, the older people begin to enjoy themselves. First they sit round the table which stands in the middle of the room under the lamp, and partake of tea and *speculaas*, until their own "surprises" begin to arrive. At ten o'clock the room is cleared, the dust-sheet which was laid down for the children's scramble is taken up, and all the papers and shavings, boxes and baskets that contained presents are removed from the floor; the table is spread with a white tablecloth; *letterbanket* and hot punch or milk chocolate are provided for the guests ; and when all have taken their seats a dish of boiled chestnuts, steaming hot, is brought in and eaten with butter and salt.

Cigars, the usual resource of Dutchmen when they do not know what to do with themselves, do not form a feature of this memorable evening (memorable for this fact also), not so much out of deference to the ladies who are in their midst as for the reason that they are too fully occupied with other and even pleasanter employments.

The personality of St. Nicholas, as now known by Dutch children, is of mixed origin, for not merely the Bishop of Lycië, but Woden, the Frisian god of the elements and of the harvest, figures largely in the legends attached to his name. Woden possessed a magic robe which enabled him when arrayed in it to go to any place in the world he wished in the twinkling of an eye. This same power is attached to the *beste tabbaard* of St. Nicholas, as may be seen from the verse addressed to him :

> " Sint Niklaas, goed, heilig man,
> Trek je beste tabberd an,
> Ryd er mee naar Amsterdam,
> Van Amsterdam naar Spanje."

[" St. Nicholas, good, holy man,
Put on your best gown,
Ride with it to Amsterdam,
From Amsterdam to Spain."]

The horse Sleipnir, on whose back Woden took his autumn ride through the world, has been converted into the horse of St. Nicholas, on which the Saint rides about over the roofs of the houses to find out where the good and where the naughty children live. In pagan days a sheaf of corn was always left out on the field in harvest-time for Woden's horse, and the children of the present day still carry out the same idea by putting a wisp of hay in their shoes for the four-footed friend of the good saint. The black servant who now always accompanies St. Nicholas is an importation from America, for the Pilgrim Fathers carried their St. Nicholas festival with them to the New Country, and some of their descendants who came to live in Holland brought *Knecht Ruprecht* with them, and so added another feature to the St. Nicholas festivity.

What the Dutch originally knew of the life and works of *Dominus Sanctus Nicolaus* was told them by the Spaniards at the time of their influence in Holland, and so it is believed that the Saint was born at Myra, in Lycië, and lived in the commencement of the fourth century, in the reign of Constantine the Great. From his earliest youth he showed signs of great piety and self-denial, refusing, it is said, even when quite a tiny child, to take food more than once a day on fast days! His whole life was devoted to doing good, and even after his death he is credited with performing many miracles. Maidens and children chiefly claim him as their patron saint, but he also guards sailors, and legend asserts that many a ship on the point of being wrecked or stranded has been saved by his timely influence. During his lifetime the circumstance took place for which he was ever afterwards recognised as the maidens' guardian. A certain man had lost all his money, and to rid himself from his miserable situation he determined to sell his three beautiful daughters for a large sum. St. Nicholas heard of his intention, and went to the man's house in the night, taking with him some of the money left him by his parents, and dropped it through a broken window-pane. The following night St. Nicholas again took a purse of gold to the poor man's house, and managed to drop it through the chimney, but when he reached the man's door on the third night it was suddenly opened from the inside, and the poor man rushed out, caught St. Nicholas by his robe, and falling down on his knees before him, exclaimed: " O Nicholas, servant of the Lord, wherefore dost thou hide thy good deeds?" and from that time forth everyone knew it was St. Nicholas who brought presents during the night.

In pictures one often sees St. Nicholas represented with the threefold gift in his hand, in the

Kermis and St. Nicholas

form of three golden apples, fruits of the tree of life. Another very well known Dutch picture is St. Nicholas standing by a tub, from which are emerging three boys. About fifty years ago such a picture was to be seen in Amsterdam on the corner house between the Dam and the Damrak, with the inscription, *Sinterklaes*. The story runs that three boys once lost their way in a dark wood, and begged a night's lodging with a farmer and his wife. While the children were asleep the wicked couple murdered them, hoping to rob them of all they had with them, but they soon discovered that the lads had no treasure at all, and so to guard against detection they salted the dead bodies and put them in the tub with the pigs' flesh. That same afternoon, while the farmer was at the market, St. Nicholas appeared to him in his episcopal robes and asked him whether he had any pork to sell. The man replied in the negative, when St. Nicholas rejoined: "What of the three young pigs in your tub?" This so frightened the farmer that he confessed his wicked deed, and implored forgiveness. St. Nicholas thereupon accompanied him to his house, and waved his staff over the meat-tub, and immediately the three boys stepped forth well and hearty, and thanked St. Nicholas for restoring them to life.

The birch rod, which naughty Dutch children have still to fear, has also a legendary origin, and is not merely an imaginary addition to the attributes of the Saint. A certain abbot would not allow the responses of St. Nicholas to be sung in his church, notwithstanding the repeated requests of the monks of his order, and he dismissed them at last with the words, "I consider this music worldly and profane, and shall never give permission for it to be used in my church." These words so enraged St. Nicholas that he came down from the heavens at night when the abbot was asleep, and, dragging him out of bed by the hair of his head, beat him with a birch rod he carried in his hand till he was more dead than alive. The lesson proved salutary, and from that day forth the responses of St. Nicholas formed a part of the service.

The St. Nicholas festival has always been kept with the greatest splendour at Amsterdam. It was there that the festival was first instituted, and the first church built which was dedicated to his name; for when Gysbrecht III., Heer van Amstel, had the Amstel dammed, many people came to live there, and houses arose up on all sides, and naturally, when the want of a church was felt, and it was built, the good Nicholas was chosen the patron Saint of the town. On his name-day masses were held in the church, and the usual Kermis observed. Booths and stalls were set out in two rows all along the Damrak, where the people of Amsterdam could buy sweets and toys for their children. Special cakes were baked in the form of a bishop, and named after

Kermis and St. Nicholas

St. Nicholas *Klaasjes*. They were looked upon as an offering dedicated to the Saint, according to the old custom of their forefathers, which can be again traced to the service of Woden.

Not only Amsterdamers, however, but people from all the neighbouring towns flocked to the St. Nicholas market, and followed the Amsterdamers' example of filling their children's shoes with cakes and toys, always telling them the old legend that St. Nicholas himself brought these presents through the chimney and put them in their shoes. During and after the Reformation this now popular festival had to bear a great deal of opposition, for authors and preachers alike agreed that it was a foolish feast, and led to superstition and idolatry. Hence the decree was issued in the year 1622 that no cakes might be baked and no Kermis held, and even the children were forbidden to put out their shoes as they were accustomed to do. But for once in a way people were sensible enough to understand that giving their children a pleasant evening had nothing to do either with superstition or idolatry, and so the festival lived on with Protestants as well as Roman Catholics, although one point was gained by the Reformers in that St. Nicholas was no longer looked upon as holy and worshipped, but was only honoured as the patron Saint and guardian of their children.

The fairs which once belonged to the festival

of St. Nicholas are no longer held in the street, at any rate in the larger towns, but the exchange of presents is as universal as ever, and the shops look as festive as shops in England do at Christmas-time. In many other ways, indeed, St. Nicholas corresponds to Christmas in other countries, and Protestants and Catholics alike observe it, although there is no religious significance in the festival. The season, too, has its special cakes and sweets. There are the flat, hard cakes, made in the shapes of birds, beasts, and fishes— the so-called *Klaasjes*—for they are no longer baked only in the form of a bishop, as they used to be. Then there is *letterbanket*, made, as the name implies, in the form of letters, so that anyone who likes can order his name in cake, and the *marsepein* (marchpane) is now made in all possible shapes, though formerly only in heart-shaped sweets, ornamented with little turtle-doves made of pink sugar, or a flaming heart on a little altar. These sweets, it is said, were invented by St. Nicholas himself when he was a bishop for the benefit and use of lovers, for St. Nicholas held the office of *hylik-maker*, and many a couple was united by him. That is why the confectioners bake *vryers* and *vrysters* of cake at St. Nicholas time. If a young man wanted to find out whether a girl cared for him, he used to send her a heart of *marsepein* and a *vryer* of cake. Should she accept this present he knew he had nothing to fear, but if she declined to accept it he knew there was no hope for him in that quarter. These large dolls of cake were usually decorated with strips of gold paper pasted over them, but this fashion has gone out of use, and has caused the death of another old custom, for it used to be a great treat for children and young people to go and help the confectioners (who sent all their customers an invitation for that evening) on the 4th of December to prepare their goods for the *étalage*. Any cake that broke while in their hands they were allowed to eat, and no doubt many did break.

It is not likely that this celebration of St. Nicholas will ever be abolished, and the shopkeepers do their best to perpetuate it by offering new attractions for the little folk every year. Figures of St. Nicholas, life-size, are placed before their windows, and some even have a man dressed like the good Saint, who goes about the streets mounted on a white steed, while behind him follows a cart laden with parcels, which have been ordered and are left in this way at the different houses. Crowds of children, singing, shouting, and clapping their hands, follow in the rear, adding to the noise and bustle of the already crowded streets, but people are too good-natured at St. Nicholas time to expostulate. Smiling faces, mirth, and jollity abound everywhere, and good feeling unites all men as brethren on this most popular of all the Dutch festivals.

CHAPTER XI

NATIONAL AMUSEMENTS

HOLLAND, like other countries, is indebted to primitive and classic times for most of its national amusements and children's games, which have been handed down from generation to generation. Many of the same games have been played under many differing Governments and opposing creeds. Hollander and Spaniard, Protestant and Catholic alike, have found common ground in those games and sports which afford so welcome a break in daily work.

Hinkelbaan, for example, found its way into the Netherlands from far Phœnicia, whose people invented it. The game of cockal, *Bikkelen*, still played by Dutch village children on the blue doorsteps of old-fashioned houses, together with *Kaatsen*, was introduced into Holland by Nero Claudius Druses, and it is stated that he laid out the first *Kaatsbaan*. The Frisian peasant is very fond of this game, and also of *Kolven*, the older form of golf, and often on a Sunday morning after church he may be seen, dressed in his velvet suit and low-buckled shoes,

National Amusements

engaged in these outdoor sports. About a century ago a game called *Malien* was universally played in South Holland and Utrecht. For this it was necessary to have a large piece of ground, at one end of which poles were erected, joined together by a porch. The ball was driven by a *Malien kolf*, a long stick with an iron head and a leather grip, and it had to touch both poles and roll through the porch. The *Malieveld* at The Hague and the *Maliebaan* at Utrecht remind one of the places in which this game was played.

In Friesland the Sunday game for youths is *Het slingeren met Dimterkoek* — throwing Deventer cake. Four persons are required to play this game. The players divide themselves into opposite parties, and play against each other. First—they toss up to see which of the parties and which of the boys shall begin. He on whom the lot falls is allowed to give his turn to his opponent, which he often does if, on feeling the cake, he notices that it is soft and likely to break easily. If, on the contrary, it is hard, he keeps the first throw for himself. Holding the cake firmly in his right hand, he takes a little run, bends backward, and with a sudden swing throws the cake forward (as one throws a stone) so that it flies away a good distance, breaking off just at the grip. This piece, called *hanslik*, or handpiece, he must keep in his hand, for if he drops it he must let his turn pass by once, and his throw is not counted. The distance of the throw is now measured and noted down, whereupon one of the opposing party takes the piece of cake and throws it, and so it goes on alternately till each has had a turn. The distances of the throws of every two boys are counted together, and the side which has the most points wins.

There are also games played only at certain seasons of the year, as the *eiergaaren* at Easter-time. This was very popular even in the sixteenth and seventeenth centuries. On Easter Monday all the village people betake themselves to the principal street of the *dorp* to watch the *eiergaarder*. At about two o'clock in the afternoon the innkeeper who provides the eggs appears upon the scene with a basket containing twenty-five. These he places on the road at equal distances of twelve feet from each other. In the middle of the road is then placed a tub of water, on which floats a very large apple, the largest he has been able to procure. Two men are chosen from the ranks of the villagers. The one is led to the tub, his hands are tied behind his back, and he is told to eat the floating apple; the other has to take the basket in his hand and pick up while running all the eggs and arrange them in the basket before the apple is eaten. He who finishes his task first is the winner, and carries off the basket of eggs as a prize. It provokes great fun to see the man trying to get hold of the floating apple, which escapes so easily from the grasp of his teeth, but some men are wise enough to push the apple against the side of the tub, and of course as soon as they have taken one bite the rest is easily eaten. When the game is over, the greater number of the villagers go and drink to the good health of the winner at the public-house, and so the innkeeper makes a good thing out of this custom also, and for a game like this it is certainly wise to refresh one's self *after* the event. Skittles and billiards are very popular with the peasant and working classes on Sunday afternoons, the only free time a labourer has for recreation. Games of chance, also, in which skill is at a minimum, are as numerous in Holland as in any other country.

Children's games naturally occupy a large share in young Netherlands life, especially outdoor romping games. Of indoor games there are very few, a fact which may, perhaps, be accounted for by the custom of allowing children to play in the streets. In former days, children of all classes played together in outdoor sports and games, and developed both their muscles and their republican character. Even Prince Frederik Hendrik (who was brother to and succeeded Prince Maurits in 1625), when at school at Leyden, mixed freely with his more humble companions, and was often mistaken for an ordinary schoolboy, and an old woman once sharply rebuked him for daring to use her boat-hook to fish his ball out of the water into which it had fallen.

Nor did she notice to whom she was speaking until a passer-by called her attention to the fact that it was the Prince, whereupon the poor old soul became so frightened that she durst not venture out of her house for weeks from imaginary fear of falling into the clutches of the law, and ending her days in prison.

Games may be divided into two classes, those played with toys and those for which no toys are needed ; but whatever the games may be they all have their special seasons. Once a man wrote an almanack on children's games, and noted down all the different sports and their seasons, but, as the poet Huggens truly said,

"De kindren weten tyd van knickeren en kooten,
 En zonder almanack en ist hen nooit ontschoten,"

which, freely translated, means that children know which games are in season by intuition, and do not need an almanack, so he might have saved himself the trouble. "The children know the time to play marbles and *kooten*, and without an almanack have not forgotten."

In the eighteenth century, driving a hoop was as popular an amusement with children as it is now, only then it was also a sport, and prizes were given to the most skilful. In fact, hoop-races were held, and boys and girls alike joined in them. They had to drive their hoops a certain distance, and the one who first reached the goal received a silver coin for a prize. This coin was fastened to the hoop as a trophy, and the more noise a hoop made while rolling over the streets the greater the honour for the owner of it, for it showed that a great many prizes had been gained. In Drenthe the popular game for boys is *Man ik sta op je blokhuis*, similar to "I am the King of the Castle," but there is also the *Windspel*. For the latter a piece of wood and a ball are necessary. The wood is placed upon a pole and the ball laid on one side of it, then with a stick the child strikes as hard as possible the other side of the piece of wood, at the same time calling "W-i-n-d," and the ball flies up into the air, and may be almost lost to sight.

Boer, lap den buis, an exciting game from a boy's point of view, is a general favourite in Gelderland and Overyssel. For this the boys build a sort of castle with large stones, and after tossing up to see who is to be "boer," the boy on whom the lot has fallen stands in the stone fortress, and the others throw stones at it from a distance, to see whether they can knock bits off it. As soon as one succeeds in doing so he runs to get back his stone, at the same time calling out "*Boer, lap den buis*," signifying that the "boer" must mend the castle. If the "boer" accomplishes this, and touches the bag before the other has picked up his stone, they change places, and the game begins anew.

Little girls of the labouring classes have not

much time for games of any sort, for they are generally required at home to act as nursemaids and help in many other duties of the home life, but sometimes on summer afternoons they bring out their younger brothers and sisters, their knitting, and a skipping-rope, which they take in turns, and so pass a few pleasant hours free from their share (not an inconsiderable one) of household cares, or in the evenings, when the younger members of the family are in bed, they will be quite happy with a bit of rope and their skipping songs, of which they seem to know many hundreds, and which might be sung with equal reason to any other game under the sun for all the words have to do with skipping.

After a long spell of rain the first fall of snow is hailed with delight, for it is a sign that frost is not far off. Jack Frost, after several preliminary appearances in December, usually pays his first long visit in January (sometimes, however, this is but a flying visit of two or three days), and, as a rule, a Dutchman may reckon on a good hard winter. As soon, therefore, as he sees the snow he thinks of the good old saying—"*Sneeuw op slik in drie dagen ys dun of dik*" (Snow on mud in three days' time, ice thin or thick). Ice is to be expected, and he gets out his skates with all speed. This is one of the few occasions when the people of the Netherlands are enthusiastic. Certainly, skating is *the* national sport. The ditches are always the first to be tried, as the water in

National Amusements 139

them is very shallow, and naturally freezes sooner than the very deep and exposed waters of river and canal, over which the wind, which is always blowing in Holland, has fair play; but when once these are frozen, then skating begins in real earnest. The tracks are all marked out by the Hollandsche Ysvereeniging, a society which was founded in 1889 in South Holland, and which the other provinces have now joined. Finger-posts to point the way are put up by this society at all cross-roads and ditches, with notices to mark the dangerous places, while the newspapers of the day contain reports as to which roads are the best to take, and which trips can be planned. For people living in South Holland the first trip is always to the Vink at Leyden, as it can be reached by narrow streams and ditches, and it is quite a sight to see the skaters sitting at little tables with plates of steaming hot soup before them. The Vink has been famous for its pea-soup many years, and has been known as a restaurant from 1768. When the Galgenwater is frozen (the mouth of the Rhine which flows into the sea at Katwyk), then the Vink has a still gayer appearance, for not only skaters, but pedestrians from Leyden and the villages round about that town, flock to this *café* to watch the skating and enjoy the amusing scenes which the presence of the ice affords them. Then the broad expanse of water, which in summer looks so deserted and gloomy as it flows silently and dreamily towards the sea, is dotted all over with tents, flags, *baanvegers*, and, if the ice is strong, even sleighs.

Among the peasant classes of South Holland it is the custom, as soon as the ice will bear, to skate to Gouda, men and women together, there to buy long Gouda pipes for the men and *Goudsche sprits* for the women, and then to skate home with these brittle objects without breaking them. As they come along side by side, the farmer holding his pipe high above his head and the woman carefully holding her bag of cakes, every passer-by knocks against them and tries to upset them, but it seldom happens that they succeed in doing so, as a farmer stands very firmly on his skates, and, as a rule, he manages to keep his pipe intact after skating many miles. The longest trip for the people of South Holland, North Holland, and Utrecht, is through these three provinces, and the way over the ice-clad country is quite as picturesque as in summer-time, the little mills, quaint old drawbridges, and rustic farmhouses losing nothing of their own charm in winter garb. All along the banks of the canals and rivers little tents are put up to keep out the wind; a roughly fashioned rickety table stands on the ice under the shelter of the matting, and here are sold all manner of things for the skaters to refresh themselves with—hot milk boiled with aniseed and served out of very sticky cups, stale biscuits, and sweet cake. The tent-holders call out their wares in the most poetical language they can muster:

National Amusements

"Leg ereis an! Leg ereis an!
In het tentje by de man;
Warme melk en zoete koek
En een bevrozen vaatedoek."

["Put up, put up
At the tent with the man;
Warm milk and sweet cake,
And a frozen dish-cloth."]

and they tell you plainly that you may expect unwashed cups, for the cloth wherewith to wipe them is frozen, as well as the water to cleanse them.

Under the bridges the ice is not always safe, and even if it has become safe the men break it up so that they may earn a few cents by people passing over their roughly constructed gangways, and so boards are laid down by the *baanvegers* for the skaters to pass over without risking their lives. Besides making these wooden bridges the *baanvegers* keep the tracks clean. Every hundred yards or so one is greeted by the monotonous cry of "*Denk ereis an de baanveger*," so that on long trips these sweepers are a great nuisance, for having to get out one's purse and give them cents greatly impedes progress. The Ice Society has, however, minimised the annoyance by appointing *baanvegers* who work for it and are paid out of the common funds, so that the members of the society who wear their badge can pass a *baanveger* with a clear conscience, while as the result of this combination you can skate over miles of good and well-swept ice without interference for the modest sum of tenpence, this being the cost of membership of the society for the whole season.

The Kralinger Plassen and the Maas near Rotterdam are greatly frequented spots for carnivals on the ice, but the grandest place for skating and ice sports of all kinds is the Zuyder Zee. In a severe winter this large expanse of ice connects instead of dividing Friesland and North Holland. Here we see the little ice-boats flying over the glossy surface as fast as a bird on the wing, and sleighs drawn by horses with waving plumes, while thousands of people flock from Amsterdam to the little Isle of Marken, and the variety of costume and colour swaying to and fro on the fettered billows of the restless inland sea makes it seem for the moment as though the Netherlander's dream had come true, and Zuyder Zee had really become once more dry land. In winter everyone, from the smallest to the greatest, gives himself up to ice sports, and even the poor are not forgotten. In some villages races are proclaimed, for which the prizes are turfs, potatoes, rice, coals, and other things so welcome to the poor in cold weather. A racer is appointed for every poor family, and where there are no sons big enough to join in the races, a young man of the better classes generally offers his services, and, when successful, hands his prize over to the family he undertook to help.

National Amusements

Skating is second nature with the Dutch, and as soon as a child can walk it is put upon skates, even though they may often be much too big for it. Moreover, when the ice is good, winter-time affords recreation for the working as well as the leisured classes, for the canals and rivers become roads, and the hard-worked errand-boys, the butchers' and the bakers' boys manage to secure many hours of delightful enjoyment as they travel for orders on skates. The milkman also takes his milk-cart round on a sledge, and the farmers skate to market, saving both time and money, for then there is no railway fare to be paid, and a really good skater goes almost as fast as a train in Holland — especially the Frisian farmers, for Frisians are renowned for their swift skating, and the most famous racer of the commencement of the nineteenth century, Kornelis Ynzes Reen, skated four miles in five minutes.

But although the ice affords, and always has afforded, so much pleasure, there are periods in history when the frost caused great anxiety to the people of the Netherlands. The cities Naarden and Dordrecht are easily reached by water, and when that is frozen it would give anyone free access to the town, and so in time of war frost was a much-dreaded thing. On one occasion this fear was realised, for when the ships of the Geuzen round about Naarden were stuck fast in the ice, and the Zuyder Zee was frozen, the enemy, armed with canoes and battle-axes, came over the ice from the Y and across the Zuyder Zee to Naarden. The best skaters among the Geuzen immediately volunteered to meet the Spaniards on the ice. They took only their swords with them, and while the ships' cannon had fair play from the bulwarks of the vessels over the heads of the Geuzen into the Spanish ranks, the Geuzen could approach them fearlessly and unmolested for a hand-to-hand fight. The Spaniards, who, besides being very heavily armed, were very bad skaters, were soon defeated, for they kept tumbling over each other. The Geuzen pursued them to Amsterdam, and then returned to their ships, where they were greeted with great enthusiasm, and, as the thaw set in the next day, they were happily saved from a renewed attack.

A CANAL IN DORDRECHT

CHAPTER XII

MUSIC AND THE THEATRE

SINGING was one of the principal social pastimes of the Dutch nation during the eighteenth and far into the nineteenth century, and the North Hollander was especially fond of vocal music. When young girls went to spend the evening at the house of a friend they always carried with them their *Liederboek*—a volume beautifully bound in tortoise-shell covers or mounted with gold or silver. The songs contained in these books were a strange mixture of the gay and grave. Jovial drinking-songs or *Kermisliedjes* would find a place next to a *Christian's Meditation on Death*. It was an *olla podrida* in which everybody's tastes were considered. Recitations were also a feature of these little gatherings.

Nowadays these national songs are rarely heard. French, Italian, and German songs have taken their place, and it is but seldom one hears a real Dutch song at any social gathering. The "people," too, seem to have forgotten their natural gift of poetry, for the only songs now heard about the streets are badly translated French or English ditties. If England brings out a comic song of questionable art, six months later that song will have made its way to Holland, and will have taken a popular place in a Dutch street musician's repertoire; it will be whistled in many different keys by butcher and baker boys, and will be heard issuing painfully from the wonderful mechanism of the superfluous concertina. For almost everyone in Holland possesses some musical instrument on which he plays, well or otherwise, when his daily work is over, or on Sunday evenings at home. And here a notable characteristic of the Dutch higher classes must be mentioned by way of contrast. Musical though they are, trained as they generally are both to play and sing well, they yet seldom exercise their gifts in a friendly, social, after-dinner way in their own homes. They become, in fact, so critical or so self-conscious that they prefer to pay to hear music rendered by recognised artists, and so a by no means inconsiderable element of geniality is lost to the social and domestic circle.

The decay of folk-song is the more regrettable, since Holland is rich in old ballads, some of which, handed down just as the people used to sing them centuries ago, are quaint, naïve, and exceedingly pretty. The melodies have all been put to modern harmonies by able composers, and published for the use of the public.

"Het daghet in het osten,
Het licht is overal,"

is a little jewel of poetic feeling, and the melody is very sweet. The story, like most of the songs of the past troublous centuries, tells of a battlefield where a young girl goes to seek her lover, but finds him dead. So, after burying him with her own white hands, with his sword and his banner by his side, she vows entrance into a convent. The story is a picture in miniature of the times, and as a piece of literature it ranks high.

Music of some sort finds a place in the homes of the poorest, and the concert, theatre, and opera are as much frequented by the humble of the land as by the wealthy and noble born. The servant class on their "evening out" frequently go to the French opera, and there is not a boy on the street but is able to whistle some tune from the great modern operas, such as *Faust*, *Lohengrin*, and other standard works. And no wonder, for the choristers in the operas walk behind fruit-carts all day long, and often call out their wares in the musical tones learnt while following their more select profession as public singers. Some, of course, cannot read a note of music, and the melodies they have to sing have to be drummed, or rather trumpeted, into their ears. To this end they are placed in a row, and a man with a large trumpet stands before them and plays the tune over and over again until they know it. In the summer-time whole parties of these Jewish youths — for Jewish they chiefly are—go about the woods on their Sabbath day singing the parts they take in the operas in the winter season, and crowds of people flock to hear them, for their voices are really well worth listening to.

Concerts are naturally not so largely patronised by the people as are operas and theatres. In the larger towns of Holland especially, theatricals take a very prominent place in popular relaxation, and even the smaller towns and villages, should they lack theatres and be unable to get good theatrical companies to pay them periodical visits, arrange for dramatic performances by local talent. The popularity of the opera may be judged from the fact that at Amsterdam, The Hague, Rotterdam, Groningen, Arnhem, and Utrecht, operas in Dutch and French are regularly given, and, occasionally, works in German and even Italian are produced. Money is scarce in Holland, the people generally have little to spare, so grand opera-houses such as are thought necessary in most European cities of any pretension to culture are impossible, and the singers can seldom count on liberal fees. But most of the best works are heard all the same — which, after all, is the principal thing—and the enjoyment and edification which result are not less genuine because of the simplicity of the properties and the humble character of the entire surroundings.

Yet outdoor music possesses a powerful attrac-

Music and the Theatre

tion for the Dutch humbler classes, as for the same classes in most, if not all, countries; and when in the summer-time there is music in the Wood at The Hague on Sunday afternoons or Wednesday evenings, the walks round about the *Societ Tent* are alive with servants and their lovers, parading decorously arm-in-arm. Happy fathers, too, with their wives and children in Sunday best, perambulate the grounds or rest on the seats amongst the trees and listen to the *Boschmuziek*. People of the better class only are members of the *Witte Societeit*, and sit inside the green paling to listen to the music and drink something meanwhile. For it is strange but true, that a Dutchman never seems thoroughly to enjoy himself unless he has liquid of some sort at hand, and never feels really comfortable without his cigar. Indeed, if smoking were abolished from places of public amusement, most Dutchmen would frequent them no more. In winter, concerts are given every other Wednesday at The Hague—and what is true of The Hague applies to Amsterdam and all other towns of any size in the country — and the Public Hall is always packed; but besides these *Diligentia* concerts there are others given by various Singing Societies, so that there is variety enough to choose from.

In the summer-time there is another attraction besides the Wood for the people of The Hague, for the season at Scheveningen opens on the 1st of June, and there is music at the Kurhaus twice a day—in the afternoon on the terrace of that building, and in the evening in the great hall inside. On Friday night is given what is called a "Symphony Concert." To this all the world flocks, for no one who at all respects himself, or esteems the opinion of society, would venture to miss it. Whether everyone understands or enjoys the high-class music given is another question, which it would be imprudent to press too urgently, but then it belongs to "education" to go to concerts, and so all enjoy it in their own way. For the townspeople and the working-classes, who have no free time during the week, concerts are given at the large Voorhout on Sunday evenings in summer, so that on that day even the busiest and poorest may enjoy recreation of a better kind than the public-house offers them, and this effort on their behalf is greatly appreciated by the people, who gladly make use of the opportunities of hearing good and popular music.

The national love of music is assiduously fostered by the Netherlands Musical Union, whose branches are to be found all over the country. Every town has musical and singing societies of some kind — private as well as public—and these make life quite endurable in winter, even in the smallest places. Nor do these *Zangvereenigingen* derive their membership exclusively from the higher classes, for the humbler folk have organisations of their own. Even the servant-girl and the day-labourer will often be found to belong to singing clubs of some kind. Music is also taught at most of the public schools, though it was long before the Government capitulated upon the point, and gave this subject a place side by side with drawing as part of the normal curriculum of the children of the people.

Happily for the musical and dramatic tastes of the nation, both the concert and the theatre are cheap amusements in Holland. As a rule, the dearest seats cost only from 3s. to 5s., while the cheapest, even in first-class houses at Amsterdam, Rotterdam, and The Hague, cost as little as sixpence. The only exceptions are when renowned artists tour the country, and even then the prices seldom exceed £1 for the best places. There is one musical event which makes a more serious call upon the purse, and it is the periodical operatic performance of the Wagner Society in Amsterdam. As a rule, two representations a year are given, and some of the best singers of Europe are invited to sing in one or other of Wagner's operas. The best Dutch orchestra plays, and chosen voices from the Amsterdam Conservatoire take part in the choruses. The scenery is worthy of Bayreuth itself, and such expense and care are bestowed upon these choice performances that, though the house is invariably filled on every occasion, the fees for admission never pay the costs, so that the musical enthusiasts of Amsterdam,

Haarlem, and The Hague regularly make up the deficit each year, which sometimes amounts to as much as £1000.

While, however, the Dutch may with truth be classed as a distinctly musical nation, they would seem to have outlived their fame in the domain of musical art. For it should not be forgotten that Holland has in this respect a distinguished history behind it. So long ago as the times of Pope Adrian I. a Dutch school of music was established under the tuition of Italian masters, and it compared favourably with the contemporary schools of other nations. Even in the ninth century Holland produced a composer famous in the annals of music in the person of the monk Huchbald of St. Amand, in Flanders. He it was who changed the notation, and arranged the time by marking the worth of each note, and he is also remembered for his *Organum*, the oldest form of music written in harmonies. It is often lamented that the compositions of to-day lack the originality which marked the earlier works. The country has none the less produced some noticeable composers during the past century. Of these J. Verhulst, W. F. G. Nicolaï, Daniël de Lange, Richard Hol, and G. Mann are best known, though of no modern composer can it be said that he has any special "*cachet*," for the younger men, fed as they are on the works of other nations, grow into their style of thinking and writing, and follow almost slavishly in their footsteps. It is unfortunate that many rising composers cannot be persuaded to publish their works. The reason is that the cost of publishing in the Netherlands is almost fabulous, and if they do publish them at all it is done in Germany. But even then the circulation is so limited, owing to the smallness of the country, that it does not repay the cost; and so they prefer to plod on unknown, or to cultivate celebrity by giving private concerts of their own works.

CHAPTER XIII

SCHOOLS AND SCHOOL LIFE

IF the Dutch peasant is not generally well educated it is not for want of opportunity, but rather because he has not taken what is offered him. For many years past a good elementary education has been within the reach of all. Even the small fees usually asked may be remitted in the case of those parents who cannot afford to pay anything, without entailing any civil disability; but attendance at school was only made compulsory by an Act which passed the Second Chamber in March, 1900, and which, at the time of writing, has just come into force. It is said that as many as sixty thousand Dutch children are getting no regular schooling. About one-half of this number live on the canal-boats, and will probably give a good deal of trouble to those who will administer the new Act; for, as we have already seen, the families that these boats belong to have no other homes and are always on the move, so that it must ever be difficult to get hold of the children, especially as their parents do not see the necessity of sending them

Schools and School Life

to school. It remains to be seen, therefore, whether any great improvement will result from the new Act, especially as private tuition may take the place of attendance at a school, and exemption is granted to those who have no fixed place of abode, and to parents who object to the tuition given in all the schools within two and a half miles of their homes. Under these conditions it seems that anyone who wishes to evade the law will have little difficulty in doing so. The canal-boat people, apparently, are exempt so long as they do not remain for twenty-eight days consecutively in the same *gemeente*, or commune.

The education provided by the State is strictly neutral in regard to religion and politics, but there are many denominational schools all over the country. Protestants call theirs "Bible schools," and Romanists call theirs "Catholic schools," and both these receive subsidies from the State if they satisfy the inspectors. Private schools also exist, but do not as a rule receive State aid. They are all, however, under State supervision and subject to the same conditions as to teachers' qualifications; and a very good rule is in force, namely, that no one may teach in Holland without having passed a Government examination.

Instruction in the elementary schools supported by the Government is in two grades, though the dividing line is not always clearly drawn. In Amsterdam, for example, there are four different grades. In the lower schools the subjects taught are, besides reading, writing, and arithmetic, grammar and history, geography, natural history and botany, drawing, singing, and free gymnastics, and the girls also learn needlework; but a large proportion of the pupils are satisfied with a more modest course, and know little more than the three R's. The children attending these schools are between six and twelve years of age, though in some rural districts few of them are less than eight years old, but according to the new law they must begin to attend when they are seven and go on until they are twelve or thirteen according to the standard attained. In the upper grade schools the same subjects are taught in a more advanced form, with the addition of universal history, French, German, and English. These languages, being optional, are taught more or less after regular school hours.

All the teachers in these schools must hold teachers' or head-teachers' certificates, to gain which they have to pass an examination in all the subjects which they are to teach except languages, for each of which a separate certificate is required. Every commune must have a school, though hitherto no one has been obliged to attend it, and lately, owing to the new Education Act, the builders have been busy in many places enlarging the schools to meet the new requirements. If there are more than forty children two masters are now necessary, and for more

Schools and School Life

than ninety there must be at least three. Ten weeks' holidays are allowed in the year, and these are to be given when the children are most wanted to help at home, in addition to which leave of absence may be granted in certain cases by the district inspectors. Holidays, therefore, vary according to the conditions of the town or village.

All schools are more or less under State control. They are divided into three classes according to the type of education which they provide. Lower or elementary education has already been dealt with. Between this and the higher education of the *Gymnasia* and Universities comes what is called *middelbaar onderwijs* — that is secondary, or rather intermediate, education. This is represented by technical or industrial schools, "Burgher night schools," and "Higher burgher schools." The first-named train pupils for various trades and crafts, more especially for those connected with the principal local industries. The course is three years or thereabouts, following on that of the elementary schools, and there is generally an entrance examination, but the conditions vary in different communes. Sometimes the instruction is free, sometimes fees are charged amounting to a few shillings a year, the cost being borne by the communes, and in a few towns there are similar schools for girls who have passed through the elementary schools. The technical classes for girls cover such subjects as fancy-work, drawing and painting of a utilitarian character, and sometimes book-keeping and dress-making. Most of them are free, but for some special subjects a small payment is required. Drawing seems to be a favourite subject, and in most of these technical schools there are classes for mechanical drawing as well as for some kind of artistic work connected with industry. In addition there are numerous art schools, some of them being devoted to the encouragement of fine art, while in others the object kept in view is the application of art to industry.

The burgher night schools, like the technical schools, are supported by the communes in which they are situated. There are about forty of them in all, and most of them are very well attended; in some cases the regular students, who are all working-men and -women, number several hundreds. The instruction is similar to that given in the technical schools; that is to say, it is chiefly practical, and local industries receive special attention. Formerly there were day schools also for working-men, on the same lines as these, but they were not a success, and the technical schools have taken their place.

Of a higher class, but still included in the term *middelbaar onderwijs*, is the " modern " education of the higher burgher schools. The majority of these schools were founded by the communes, the rest by the State, but internally they are all alike, and all are inspected by commissioners appointed by the Government for the purpose. Pupils enter at twelve years of age, and must pass an entrance examination, which, like nearly every examination in Holland, is a Government affair. Having passed this, they attend school for five years, as a rule, but at some of these institutions the course lasts only three years. In some degree the higher burgher schools correspond to the modern side of an English school: at least the subjects are much the same, embracing mathematics, natural science, modern languages, and commercial subjects; and no Latin or Greek is taught. The education is wholly modern and practical, with the object of preparing pupils for commercial life. There are higher burgher schools for girls as well as for boys, at which nearly the same education is provided.

A great advantage of these schools is that they are very cheap; at the most expensive the yearly fees amount to a little more than thirty pounds, but at the majority they only come to four or five. To teach in such schools as these one must have a diploma or a University degree. A separate diploma is necessary for each subject, and the examination is not easy. Even a foreigner who wishes to teach his own language must pass the same examination as a Dutchman. No difference is made between the masters at the boys' schools and the ladies who teach the girls; exactly the same diplomas are required in both cases.

The *Gymnasia* to which allusion has been made are classical schools, which prepare boys for the Universities. The age of entry is the same as at the modern schools, twelve; but the course is longer, as a rule covering six years instead of five, and at the end of this course comes a Government examination, the passing of which is a necessary preliminary to a University degree. The *Gymnasia* were founded by an Act of Parliament, but are supported by the communes, which in this case are the larger towns, but they are assisted as a rule by a Government grant. The fees are very small, only about £8 a year.

There are a few private and endowed schools, which may send up candidates for the same examinations as are taken by the pupils of the State schools, and it is among these that we find the only boarding schools in the country. Some of these have certain privileges; for instance, the headmaster may engage assistants who do not hold diplomas, which makes it easier for him to get native teachers for modern languages; but in the State schools proper, the selection of undermasters does not rest with the head, or director, as he is called, at all. Foreign teachers are not very plentiful, as the diplomas are not easy to get, and a native, who has to re-learn much of his own language from a Dutch point of view, has little or no advantage over a Dutchman in the examinations.

No sketch of Dutch schools would be complete

Schools and School Life

without some reference to the way in which modern languages are studied, for this is the most striking feature in the national education, and is of great importance when we are considering the national life and character of Holland. Former generations of Dutchmen won a place among the "learned nations" by their knowledge of the classical languages; and their descendants seem to have inherited the gift of tongues, but make a more practical use of it. French, German, English, and Dutch, which go by the name of *de vier Talen*, or "the four languages," have taken the place of Greek and Latin. In the *Gymnasia* every pupil learns to speak them as a matter of course, and in the higher burgher schools the same languages receive special attention, with a view to commercial correspondence. Even in the upper elementary schools, boys and girls are taught some or all of them. A boy entering one of the higher schools at the age of twelve or thirteen generally has some knowledge of, at least, one foreign language, acquired either at an elementary school, or at home, and he is never shy of displaying that knowledge. If his parents are well off, he has probably learned to speak French or English in the nursery, and it sometimes happens that he even speaks Dutch with a French or an English accent, having been brought up on the foreign language and acquired his native tongue later. German as a rule is not begun so soon, the idea being that its resemblance to Dutch makes it easier, which is no doubt true to a certain extent. The result, however, is very often that the easiest language of the three is the one least correctly spoken.

As in all Continental countries, there is nothing in Holland corresponding to the English public school system. The *Gymnasia* prepare boys for the Universities, and the higher burgher schools train them for commercial life and some professions, somewhat in the same way as English modern schools, but there the resemblance ends. As a rule, a Dutch boy's school life is limited to the hours he spends at lessons; the rest of the day belongs rather to home life. There are a few boarding schools in Holland, but the life in such schools in the two countries is different in almost every respect. The size of the schools may have something to do with this, though by itself it is not enough to account for the difference. A Dutch head-master once drew my attention to the lack of tradition in his own and other schools in the country, and expressed a hope that time might work a change. At present there is little sign of such a change. Tradition has hardly had time to grow up yet, for few of the existing schools are much more than twenty years old, and its growth is retarded by the small numbers, which make any widespread freemasonry among old boys impossible. But there is another and more serious obstacle. The uniform control which the Government exercises over all schools alike, State, endowed, or private, whatever advantages it may have, certainly hinders the development of that individuality which makes "the old school," to many an English boy, something more than a place where he had lessons to do and was prepared for examinations.

A rough sketch of the inside of a Dutch school will doubtless be of interest. One of the few endowed schools in Holland may be taken as fairly typical of its class, but not of the State schools, though it competes with these and combines the classical and modern courses. It lies in the country, near a small village, and in this respect also differs from the *Gymnasia* and higher burgher schools, which are all situated in the larger towns.

One of the first things which attracts notice is the large number of masters. It seems at first that there are hardly enough boys to go round. This is due to the law which requires that every master must be qualified to teach his particular subject either by a University degree or by an equivalent diploma. Few hold more than two diplomas, and consequently much of the teaching is done by men who visit this and other schools two or three times a week. In this particular foundation the three resident masters are foreigners, but such an arrangement is exceptional. Classes seldom include more than half a dozen boys, and very often pupils are taken singly, and therefore each boy receives a good deal of individual attention. Such a school is divided into six forms or classes, but not for teaching purposes ; the day's work is differently arranged for each boy, and these classes merely record the results of the last examination. Some of the lessons last for an hour, but the rest are only three-quarters of an hour long ; they make up in number, however, what they lack in length, amounting to about nine and a half hours a day. Owing to the time being so much broken up, it may be doubted whether the amount of work done is any greater here than in an average English school where the aggregate of working hours is considerably less. Amongst our Dutch friends, however, and there may be others who share their opinion, the general belief is that English schoolboys learn very little except athletics.

With regard to sports and pastimes, these are the only schools in which any interest is taken or encouragement given therein. Football is played here on most half-holidays during the winter, and sometimes on Sunday, and occasionally its place is taken by hockey. It must be admitted that the standard of play is not very high in either game, though many of the boys work hard and, with better opportunities, might develop into high-class players ; but as there are only about thirty boys in the school, competition for places in the teams is not very keen. Rowing has lately been introduced, not to the advantage of the football eleven. It may be remarked, by the way, that only Association football is played in Holland; the Rugby game is strictly barred by head-masters and parents as too dangerous. Attempts have been made to introduce cricket, but the game meets with little encouragement. There is a lawn-tennis court, however, which is constantly in use during the summer term. Bicycling is very popular, not only here but in Holland generally; in fact, most of the boys seem to prefer this form of exercise to any of the games which have been mentioned.

Whether at work or play, all the boys are under the constant supervision of one or other of the resident masters, and the head is not far off. A few of the seniors are allowed to go outside the grounds when they please, but the rest may only go out under the charge of a master. In spite of this apparently strict supervision, however, there is not much real discipline. Corporal punishment is not allowed; both public opinion and the law of the land are against it. Other punishments, such as detention and impositions, are ineffectual, and are generally regarded by the culprit as unjustly interfering with his liberty. Consequently the masters have not much hold over the boys, who might, if they chose, perpetrate endless mischief without fear of painful consequences so long as they did nothing to warrant expulsion; but the young Hollander does not appear to have much enterprise in that direction. Perhaps he is sometimes kept out of mischief by his devotion to the fragrant weed, for he generally learns to smoke at a tender age, with his parents' consent, and no exception is taken to his cigar except during lessons; but it is certainly startling to see the boys smoking while playing their games, as well as on all other possible occasions.

A large proportion of the boys at the *Gymnasia*, perhaps the majority of them, pass on to the Universities, some to qualify for the learned professions, others because it is the fashion in Holland as in other countries for young men who have no intention of following any profession to spend a few years at a University in search of pleasure and experience ; but the experience in this case is peculiar and unique.

CHAPTER XIV

THE UNIVERSITIES

AS to the Universities themselves, it is not necessary to consider them separately, as all four of them, Leyden, Groningen, Utrecht, and Amsterdam, are alike in constitution. They are not residential, there are no beautiful buildings, there are no rival colleges, no tutors or proctors, and no " gate "; nor are they independent corporations like Oxford and Cambridge and Durham, for, though they retain some outward forms which recall a former independence, they are now maintained and managed entirely by the State, which pays the professors and provides the necessary buildings. The subjects to be taught and the examinations to be held in the various faculties are laid down by statute. Consequently the Universities show the same want of individuality as the schools, and, to an outsider at least, there seems to be nothing of the " Alma Mater " about them under the present *régime*, and no real ground for preferring any one of them to the others. At the same time, fathers usually send their sons to the Universities at which they themselves have studied, except when they and the professors happen to hold very different political opinions, but such a custom may be due as much to the national love of order and regularity as to any real attachment to a particular University. As to the political opinions of professors, their influence on the students cannot be very great in the majority of cases, being limited to the effect produced by lectures, for there is no social intercourse between teacher and taught. The professors, though very learned men, do not enjoy any great social standing, and the title does not carry with it anything like the same rank as in some other countries.

The system on which these Universities work may be a sound and logical one so far as it goes, and more up-to-date than the English residential system, which its enemies deride as mediæval and monastic; but it is a cast-iron system, designed with the object of preparing men for examinations, and one which does nothing to discover promising scholars or to encourage original work and research among those who have taken their degrees, or, according to the Dutch phrase, have gained their "promotion." There are no scholarships, nor anything that might serve the same purpose, though some such institution could hardly find a more favourable soil than that of Holland. Instruction of a very learned and thorough character is offered to those who will and can receive it, and that is all. The

The Universities

classes are open to all who pay the necessary fees, which are trifling, though the degree of Doctor may only be granted to those who have passed the *Gymnasium* final or an equivalent examination, and, provided he makes these payments, a student is free to do as he pleases, so far as his University is concerned.

Discipline there is none, except in very rare cases, when the law provides for the expulsion of offenders ; only theological candidates are indirectly restrained from undue levity by having to get a certificate of good conduct at the end of their course. There is no chapel to keep, for the student's religion and morals are entirely his own concern; there are no " collections," for if a man does not choose to read he injures no one but himself by his idleness ; and there is no Vice-Chancellor's Court, for, in theory, students are on the same footing as other people before the law, though in practice the police seldom interfere with them more than they can help. It is not surprising that young men not long from school should sometimes abuse such exceptional freedom, but their ideas of enjoyment are rather strange in foreign eyes. One of their favourite amusements seems to be driving about the town and neighbourhood in open carriages. On special occasions all the members of a club turn out, wearing little round caps of their club colours, and accompanied as likely as not by a band, and drive off in a procession to some neighbouring town, where they dine ; in the night or next morning they return, all uproariously drunk, singing and shouting, waving flags and flinging empty wine-bottles about the road. I do not wish to imply that all Dutch students behave in this way, but such exhibitions are unfortunately not uncommon, and show to what lengths " freedom " is permitted to go.

There is a limit, however, even to the liberty of students, as appears from the following anecdote. One of these young men gave a wine-party in his lodgings, and someone proposed, by way of a lark, to wake up a young woman who lived in the house opposite, and fetch her out of bed, so a rocket was produced and fired through the open window. The bombardment had the desired effect, but it also set the house on fire, and the joker's father was called on to make good the damage. Then the police took the matter up, and the culprit got several weeks' imprisonment for arson, after which he returned to the University and resumed his interrupted studies. There was no question of rustication, as the court simply inflicted the penalty laid down in the Code, and there was no other authority that had power to interfere in the matter at all.

As may well be imagined, students are not generally popular with the townsfolk, who resent the unequal treatment of the two classes, not because they wish for the same measure of licence, but because anything like rowdiness contrasts

The Universities

strongly with their own habits; and extravagance, not an uncommon failing among students in Holland or elsewhere, is absolutely repugnant to the average Dutch citizen. This feeling of resentment seems to be growing, and has already had some slight effect upon the civil authorities; if the students find some day that they have lost their privileged position, they will have only themselves to thank, and certainly the change will do them no harm.

But though a certain number go to the Universities merely to amuse themselves or to be in the fashion, most of them work well, even if they do not attend lectures regularly all through their course. In some faculties private coaching offers a quicker and easier way to "promotion" than the more orthodox one through the class-rooms. No doubt there are some who are in no hurry to leave the attractions of student life, but not many cling to them so persistently as a certain Dutch student, to whom a relative bequeathed a liberal allowance, to be paid him as long as he was studying for his degree. He became known as "the eternal student," to the great wrath of the heirs who waited for the reversion of his legacy. For most men the ordinary course is long enough, for it averages perhaps six or seven years, though there is no fixed time, and candidates may take the examinations as soon as they please. The nominal course—that is, the time over which the lectures extend—varies in the different faculties, from four years in law to seven or eight in medicine, but very few men manage, or attempt, to take a degree in law in four years. The other faculties are theology, science, including mathematics, and literature and philosophy.

The degree of Doctor is given in these five faculties, and to obtain it two examinations must be passed, the candidate's and the doctoral. After passing the latter a student bears the title *doctorandus* until he has written a book or thesis and defended it *viva voce* before the examiners. He is then " promoted " to the degree, a ceremony which generally entails, indirectly, a certain amount of expense. It appears to be the correct thing for the newly-made doctor to drive round in state, adorned with the colours of his club and attended by friends gorgeously disguised as lackeys, and leave copies of his book at the houses of the professors and his club-fellows, after which he, of course, celebrates the occasion in the invariable Dutch fashion, with a dinner. Many students, however, are not qualified to try for a degree, not having been through the *Gymnasia*, and others do not wish to do so. Sometimes the candidate's examination qualifies one to practise a profession, and is open to all; in other cases, in the faculty of medicine for example, it gives no qualification, and is only open to candidates for the degree, but then there is another, a "professional" examination, for those who do not aim at the ornamental title.

The cost of living at the Universities naturally depends very much on the student's tastes and habits. He pays to the University only 200 florins (£16 13s. 4d.) a year for four years, after which he may attend lectures free of charge, so the minimum annual expenditure is small; but it should be borne in mind that the course is about twice as long as in England. A good many students live with their families, which is cheaper than living in lodgings ; and as nearly all classes are represented, there is a considerable difference in their standards of life. Some are certainly extravagant, as in all Universities, which tends to raise prices, but, on the other hand, many of them are men whose parents can ill afford the expense, but are tempted by the value which attaches to a University career in Holland, and these bring the average down. Between these two extremes there are plenty who do very well on £150 or so a year, and £200 is probably considered a sufficiently liberal allowance by parents who could easily afford a larger sum. Even the students' corps need not lead to any great expense, as it consists of a number of minor clubs, and nearly everyone joins it, so that the pace is not always the same ; students who wish to keep their expenses down naturally join with friends who are similarly situated, leaving the more extravagant clubs to the young bloods who have plenty of money to spare.

The corps is the only tie which holds the students together where there are no colleges and athletics play but a very small part. Each University has its corps, to which all the students belong except a few who take no part in the typical student life, and are known as the *boeven*, or "knaves." A Rector and Senate are elected annually from among the members of four or five years' standing to manage the affairs of the corps. In order to become a member, a freshman, or "green," as he is called in Holland, has to go through a rather trying initiation, which lasts for three or four weeks. Having given in his name to the Senate, he must call on the members of the corps and ask them to sign their names in a book, which is inspected by the Senate from time to time, and at each visit he comes in for a good deal of "ragging," for, as he may not go away until he has obtained his host's signature, he is completely at the mercy of his tormentors. If he does not obey their orders implicitly and give any information they may require about his private affairs, he is likely to have a bad time, but as long as he is duly submissive he is generally let off with a little harmless fooling. One "green," a shy and retiring youth, who did not at all relish the impertinent inquiries which were made into his morals and family history, was made to stand at the window and give a full and particular account of himself to the passers-by, with interesting details supplied by the company. Sometimes, however, the joking is more brutal and less amusing. For instance, as a punishment for shirking the bottle, the victim was compelled to kneel on the floor with a funnel in his mouth, while his tormentors poured libations down his throat.

When the " green time " is over the new members of the corps are installed by the Rector, and drive round the town in procession, finishing up, of course, with a club dinner. The corps has its headquarters in the Students' Club, which corresponds more or less to the " Union " at an English University, though differing from the latter in two important respects : first, there are no debates, and secondly, the members are exclusively students, for, as I have already noticed, there is no social intercourse between the professors and their pupils. The reading-rooms at the club are a favourite lounge of a great many of the students, but it must be admitted that the literature supplied there is not always of a very wholesome kind, seeing that it includes " realism " of the most daring description, with illustrations to match, and obscene Parisian comic papers. Every member of the corps also belongs to one of the minor clubs of which it is made up, and which are apparently nothing more than messes, very often with only a dozen members, or less.

A few sport clubs exist, also under the control of the corps, but they do not play a very prominent part, for the taste for athletic exercises is confined to a small minority. Considering the small number of players, the proficiency attained in the exotic games of football and hockey is surprisingly high. The rowing is even better, and attracts a large number, being perhaps more suited to the physical characteristics of the race than those games for which agility is more necessary than weight and strength. Boat-races are held annually between the several Universities, in which the form of the crews is generally very good. If I am not mistaken, some of the Dutch crews that have rowed at Henley represented University clubs. The typical student, however, though well enough endowed with bone and muscle, has no ambition whatever to become an athlete, or to submit to the fatigue and self-denial of training. Probably the way he lives and his aversion to athletics, more than the length of his course of study, account for his elderly appearance, for he is not only obviously older than the average undergraduate, but begins to look positively middle-aged both in face and figure almost before he has done growing.

Before leaving the subject of the students' corps, mention must be made of the great carnival which each corps holds every five years to commemorate the foundation of its University. The *Lustrum-Maskerade*, which is the chief item in the week of festivities, is a historical pageant representing some event in the mediæval history of Holland. The chief actors are chosen from among the wealthiest of the students, and spare no trouble or expense in preparing their

The Universities

get-up, while the minor parts are allotted to the various clubs within the corps, each club representing a company of retainers or men-at-arms in the service of one of the mock princes or knights. For six days the players retain their gorgeous costumes and act their parts, even when excursions are made in the neighbourhood in company with the friends and relatives who come to join in the commemoration, and the mixture of mediæval and modern costumes in the streets has a somewhat ludicrous effect. On the first day the visitors are formally welcomed by the officers of the corps. Former students of all ages meet their old comrades, and the men of each year, after dining together, march together to the garden or park where the reception is held. Anything less like the usual calm and serious demeanour of these seniors than the way in which they dance and sing through the town is not to be imagined, for the oldest and most sedate of them are as wildly and ludicrously enthusiastic as the youngest student; and their arrival at the reception, with bands of music, skipping about and roaring student-songs like their sons and grandsons, is, to say the least, comical. But the occasion only comes once in five years, and they naturally make the most of it.

The next day the Masquerade takes place, beginning with a procession to the ground, and is repeated two or three times before huge crowds of spectators, for the townsmen are as excited as the students and the relatives, at least on the first two days. Great pains are always taken to ensure historical correctness in every detail, and the leading parts are often admirably played, and it must be the unromantic dress of the lookers-on that spoils the effect and makes one think of a circus. If only the crowd could be brought into harmony with the masqueraders in the matter of clothes the illusion might be complete; as it is, one can hardly imagine for a moment that the knights who charge so bravely down the lists mean to do one another any serious damage. A tournament is very often the subject of the pageant, or an important part of it, or sometimes a challenge and single combat are introduced as a sort of *entr'acte*. For the last four days of the feast there is no fixed order of procedure; balls, concerts, garden-parties, and so on are arranged as may be most convenient, while the intervals are spent in visits, dinners, and drives. Not until the end of the week does any student lay aside his gay costume and resume the more prosaic garments of his own times. All through the week the influence of the corps, which is the life of the University from the student's point of view, is manifest in the collective character of all the festivities, everything being done either by the corps itself or under its direction. From a comparison of this celebration with "Commencement" week we can, perhaps, gather a very fair idea of the typical points of difference between the students of Holland and of England.

CHAPTER XV

ART AND LETTERS

THE art of a country is ever in unity with the character of the people. It reflects their ideas and sentiments; their history is marked in its progress or decline; and it shows forth the influences that have been at work in the minds and very life of the nation from which it springs. If this is true of all countries, it is nowhere so visibly true as in Holland. There art underwent the most decided changes during the various periods of war and armed peace through which the little country passed. It may truly be said that " the first smile of the young Republic was art, for it was only after the revolt of the Dutch against the Spanish . . . that painting reached a high grade of perfection." One is accustomed to take it for granted too readily that the glory of Dutch art lies in the past; that the works and fame of a Van Eyck, a Rubens, Rembrandt, Van Dyck, and Ruysdaël sum up Holland's contribution to the art of the world, and that this chapter of its history, like the chapters which deal with its maritime supremacy, its industrial greatness, and its struggles for liberty, is closed forever. Nothing could be farther from the fact. Dutch art was never more virile, more original, more self-conscious than to-day, when it is represented by a band of men whose genius and enthusiasm recall the great names of the past. Professor Richard Muther has well said, in his *History of Modern Painting*, that, " So far from stagnating, Dutch art is now as fresh and varied as in the old days of its glory."

The Dutch painters of the present day include, indeed, quite a multitude of men of the very first rank, and some of them, like the three brothers Maris, are unexcelled. Jacob Maris, who died so recently as 1890, was known for his splendid landscapes, and still more for his town pictures and beach scenes. Willem Maris has a partiality for meadows in which cattle are browsing in tranquil content. Thys Maris has a very different style. He paints grey and misty figures and landscapes all hazy and scarcely visible. His love of the obscure and the suggestive led to the common refusal of his portraits by patrons, who complained that they lacked distinctness. No painter, however, commands such large prices as he, and from £2000 to £3000 is no rare figure for his canvases.

H. W. Mesdag is Holland's most celebrated sea-painter. He pictures the ever-rolling ocean with marvellous power, and carries the song of the waves and the cry of the wild sea-birds into his great paintings, which speak to one of the life and toil of the fishermen, the never-weary waters, and the ever-varying aspects of sea and sky. In this domain he is unrivalled, and he has certainly done some magnificent work. Mesdag has an exhibition of his own works every Sunday morning in his studio at The Hague, and anyone who wishes is allowed to visit it, while for the general public's benefit there is the Mesdag Panorama in the same town.

Mauve, who died in 1887, was best known for his pastoral scenes. His pictures of sheep on the moors and fens recall pleasant memories of summer days and sunny hours.

Josef Israëls went largely to the life of fishermen for his motives, though one of his best-known works is that noble one, *David before Saul*.

Bosboom one naturally associates with church interiors, wonderfully well done; Blommers, Artz, and Bles, likewise paint interiors, the first two choosing their subjects by preference from the houses of the working classes, while Bles confines himself to the dwellings of the wealthy.

Bisschop is unquestionably the best of the Dutch portrait-painters, though his still life is considered even more artistic than his portraits. The foremost of the lady portrait and figure painters is Therese Schwartze, who, like Josselin de Jong, often takes Queen Wilhelmina as a grateful subject for her brush.

The foregoing may be regarded as painters of the old school, though every one has so much originality as to be virtually the initiator of a distinct direction. The newer schools are represented by men like J. Toorop, Voerman, Verster, Camerlingh Onnes, Bauer, and Hoytema.

Toorop is the well-known symbolist. His style is Oriental rather than Dutch, and his topics for the most part are mystical in character. He is famous also for his decorative art. This many-sided man is probably the greatest artist soul in Holland. He is expert in almost every domain of art. Etching, pastel and water-colour drawing, oil-painting, wood-cutting, lithography, working in silver, copper, and brass, and modelling in clay, belong equally to his accomplishments, though as a painter he is, of course, best known.

Voerman, once known for his minutely painted flowers, is now a pronounced landscape painter. His cloud studies are marvellous, though perhaps the landscape colours are somewhat hard and overdone in the effort to produce the desired effects. He paints, as a rule, the rolling cumulus, and is one of the first of the younger artists.

Verster is known best for his impressionist way of painting flowers in colour patches, though he has now taken to the minute and mystical method of representing them.

Onnes, like Toorop, is a decided mystic, and there is a vein of mysticism in all his paintings. He is famous for his light effects in glass and pottery, and has especially a wonderful knack of painting choirs in churches all in a dreamy light.

Bauer is better known, perhaps, by his drawings and etchings than by his paintings. He paints with striking beauty old churches, temples, and mosques, generally the exteriors, and the effect of his minute work is wonderful. Bauer is also one of the finest of Dutch decorative artists.

Hoytema is known for his illustrations. Animal life is his forte, especially owls and monkeys.

Among other younger painters who, though not yet of European reputation, may still be classed with many of the older generation, are Jan Veth and H. Haverman, both of whom excel in portraits. The lady artists who have best held their own with the stronger sex include, in addition to those named, Mme. Bilders van Bosse, who paints woods and leafy groves with striking power ; and the late Mme. Vogels-Roozeboom, who found her inspiration in the flora of Nature. In her day (she died in 1894) she was the first of floral painters, and whenever she raised her brush the finest of flowers rose up as at the touch of a magic wand. Second to her, though not so well known by far, came Mlle. W. van der Sande Bakhuizen.

The Dutch are not only a nation of painters, but a nation of picture-lovers, though in Holland, as in other countries, one not seldom sees upon walls from which better would be expected tawdry art, about which all that can be said is that it was bought cheap. The country possesses a number of good public galleries, and much is done in this way and by the frequent exhibition of paintings to foster the love of the artistic. The principal exhibitions are those of the Pulchri Studio and the Kunst-kring (Art Circle) at The Hague, and the "Arti et Amicitia" at Rotterdam. To become a working member of the Pulchri Studio is counted a great honour, for the artists who are on the committee are very particular as to whom they admit into their circle, and they ruthlessly blackball anyone who is at all "amateurish" or who does not come up to their high standard. For this reason it is that so many of the younger artists give exhibitions of their own works as the only way of getting them at all known.

Sculpture is not much practised in Holland. It would seem to be an art belonging almost entirely to Southern climes, although there was a time when the Dutch modelled busts and heads from snow. The monument of Piet Hein was originally made of snow, and so much did it take the fancy of the people of Delftshaven, the place of his birth, that they had a stone monument erected for him on the place where the one of snow had stood. It is only recently, however, that sculpture has been re-introduced into Holland as a fine art, and those artists who have taken it up need hardly fear competition with their brethren of other Continental countries, for their names are already on every tongue. The first amongst those who have shown real power is Pier Pander, the cripple son of a Frisian mat-plaiter, who came over from Rome (where he had gone to complete his studies) at the special invitation of the Queen to model a bust of the Prince Consort, Duke Hendrik of Mecklenburg-Schwerin. Other notable sculptors are Van Mattos, Odé, Bart de Hove, and Van Wyck.

There is also another art which is in considerable vogue, and in which much good work has been done—that of wood-carving. In this the painter and illustrator Hoytema has shown considerable skill. Needless to say, Holland is also as famous now as ever for its pottery. Delft ware was ever the fame of the Dutch nation, though the Rosenbach and Gouda pottery is now gaining approval. It may be doubted, however, whether the love for the latter is altogether without affectation. One is inclined to believe that many of its admirers are enthusiastic to order. They admire because the leading authorities assure them it is their duty so to do.

The Netherlands, though very limited in area and small in population, can also boast of having contributed much that is excellent to the literature of the world, and in its roll of famous literary men are to be found names which would redeem any country from the charge of intellectual barrenness. Spinoza, Erasmus, and Hugo de Groot (Grotius), to name no others, form a trio whose influence upon the thought of the world, and upon the movements which make for human progress, has been beyond estimation, and which still belongs to-day to the imperishable inheritance of the race.

As illustrating the world-wide fame of Hugo de Groot it is interesting to note that on the occasion of the Peace Conference held at The Hague in 1899 the American representatives invited all their fellow-delegates to Delft, and there, in the church of his burial, papers were read in which the claim of the great thinker to perpetual honour was brought to the memories of the assembled spokesmen of the civilised world.

It is with the modern literature and literary movements of Holland, however, that these pages must concern themselves, and for practical purposes we may confine ourselves principally to the latter part of the completed century. For the early part of the nineteenth century was by no means prolific in literary achievement, and does not boast of many great names, if one disregards the writers whose lives linked that century with its predecessor, like Betjen Wolff and Agatha Deken. When, in 1814-15, Holland again became a separate kingdom, that important event failed to mark a new era in Dutch literature. Strange to say, though the political changes of the time powerfully influenced the sister arts of music and painting, which show strong traces of the transition of that crisis in the nation's history, upon literature they had no effect whatever. Before 1840 no very brilliant writers came to the front, though the period was not without notable names, such as Willem Bilderdijk, Hendrik C. Tollens, and Isaäc da Costa, all of whom possessed a considerable vogue. Bilderdijk's chief claim to fame is the fact that he wrote over 300,000 lines of verse, and regarded himself as the superior of Shakespeare; Tollens had a name for rare patriotism, and wrote many fine historical poems and ballads; while Da Costa, who was a converted Jew, had to the last, in spite of a considerable popularity as a poet, to contend with the oftentimes fatal shafts of ridicule.

A new period opened, however, about 1840, in the *Gids* movement promoted by E. J. Potgieter and R. C. Bakhuizen van den Brink, who were editors of the *Gids* and the severest of literary critics. The *Gids* was the Dutch equivalent of the *Edinburgh Review* under Jeffrey, and its criticisms were so much dreaded by the nervous Dutch author of the day that the magazine received the name of "The Blue Executioner," blue being the colour of its cover. If, however, Potgieter and Bakhuizen were unsparing in the use of the tomahawk, the service which they rendered to Dutch letters by their drastic treatment of crude and immature work was healthy and lasting in influence, for it undoubtedly raised the tone and standard of literary work, both in that day and for a long time to come, and so helped to establish modern Dutch literature on a firm basis. Perhaps the foremost figure in the literary revival which followed was Conrad Busken Huet, unquestionably the greatest Dutch critic of the last century, whose book, *Literary Criticisms and Fancies*, which contains a discriminating review of all writers from Bilderdijk forward, is essential to a thorough study of Dutch literature during the nineteenth century. Huet also emancipated literature from the orthodoxy in thought which had characterised the earlier Dutch writers, especially by his novel *Lidewyde*.

No novelist has more truly reflected the old-fashioned ideas and simple home life of Holland than Nicholas Beets, who still lives and even writes occasionally, though almost a nonagenarian. His *Camera Obscura*, which has been translated into English, entitles Beets to be recognised as the Dickens of Holland, and his two novels, *De Familie Stastoc* and *De Familie Kegge*, are familiar to every Dutchman. The historical novelists, Jacob van Lennep and Mrs. Bosboom Toussaint, should not be overlooked.

One of the foremost Dutch poets of the century is Petrus Augustus de Génestet. Although he is not free from rhetoric, and frequently uses old and worn-out similes, his general view of things is wider and his feeling deeper than those of any of his contemporaries in verse. The contrast, for example, between him and Carel Vosmaer, though they belong to the same period, is very striking, for while the poetry of Génestet is full of feeling and ideality, that of Vosmaer is unemotional; and though he dresses his thoughts in beautiful words, the impression left upon the mind after reading his poetry is that which might be left after looking at a gracefully modelled piece of marble—it is fine as art, but cold and dead, and so awakens no responsive sympathy in the mind of the beholder.

But the greatest of modern Dutch authors, and the one who may be termed the forerunner of the renaissance of 1880, was E. Douwes Dekker, who died thirteen years ago. Dekker had an eventful career. He went to the Dutch Indies at the age of twenty-one, and there spent some seventeen years in official life, gradually rising to the position of Assistant Resident of Lebac. While occupying that office his eyes were opened to the defective system of government existing in the Colonies, and the abuses to which the natives were subjected. He tried to interest the higher officials on behalf of the subject races, but as all his endeavours proved unavailing he became disheartened, and, resigning his post, returned to Holland with the object of pleading in Government circles at home the cause which he had taken so deeply to heart. As a deaf ear was still turned to all his entreaties he decided, as a last resource, to appeal for a hearing at the bar of public opinion. He entered literature, and wrote the stirring story *Max Havelaar*, in which he gave voice to the wrongs of the natives and the callous injustices perpetrated by the Colonial authorities. The book made a great sensation, and has unquestionably had very beneficial results in opening the public's eyes to some of the more glaring defects of Colonial administration.

In 1880, Dutch literature entered upon an entirely new phase. The chief authors of the movement then begun were Lodewyk van Deyssel, Albert Verwey, and Willem Kloos, who in the monthly magazine, *De Nieuwe Gids*, exercised by their trenchant criticisms the same beneficial and restraining influence upon the literature of the day as Potgieter and Bakhuizen did forty years before. The columns of the *Nieuwe Gids* were only opened to the very best of Dutch authors, and any works not coming up to the editors' high ideas of literary excellence were unmercifully "slated" by these competent critics. Independence was the prominent characteristic of the authors of the period. They shook themselves free from the old thoughts and similes, and created new paths, in which their minds found freer expression. The new thoughts demanded new words; hence came about the practice of word-combination, which was in direct defiance of the conservative canons of literary style which had hitherto prevailed; so that nowadays almost every author adds a new vocabulary of his own to the Dutch language, so enhancing the charm of his own writings and adding to the literary wealth of the nation in general.

The poetess whom Holland to-day most delights

Art and Letters

to honour is Helena Lapidoth Swarth, whose works increase in worth and beauty every year. Her command of the Dutch language and her power of wresting from it literary resources which are unattainable by any other writer have made her the admiration of all critics of penetration. Louis Couperus is also another living poet of mark, who, however, does not confine himself to formal versification, for his prose is also poetry. His best works are *Eline Vere*, the first book he wrote, and the characters in which are said to have been all taken from life, and his novels *Majesty* and *Universal Peace*, which have gained for him a European reputation, for they have been translated into most modern languages.

Women authors who have written works with a special tendency are Cornelie Huygens, who is known particularly by her novel *Barthold Margan*; Mrs. Goekoop de Jong, who champions the cause of women's rights; and Anna de Savornin Lohman, who, in a striking book entitled, *Why Question Any Longer?* has written very bitterly against the political conditions of the circle of society in which she moves.

While the authors of the present day are beneficially leavening popular opinion by inculcating higher and healthier sentiments, there are also authors in Holland, as elsewhere, who debase good metal, and write from a purely material standpoint. To this class of authors belong Marcellus Emants, and Frans Netcher.

Of Dutch dramatic writers, Herman Heyermans is one of the most noteworthy, and some of his plays have been translated into French, and produced in Paris theatres.

It is a great drawback to literary effort in Holland that the *honoraria* paid to authors are so low that most writers who happen not to be pecuniarily independent—and they are the majority—are unable to make a tolerable subsistence at home by the pen alone, and are obliged to contribute to foreign publications, and some even resort to teaching. Many Dutch authors of high rank write anonymously in English, French, and German magazines, and probably earn far more in that way than by their contributions to Dutch ephemeral literature, for the ordinary fee for a sheet of three thousand words — which is the average length of a printed sheet in a Dutch magazine—is only forty francs.

The pity is that Dutch literature itself is not known as well as it deserves to be, for anyone who takes the trouble to master the Dutch language will find himself well repaid by the treasures of thought which are contained in the modern authors of Holland.

CHAPTER XVI

THE DUTCH AS READERS

ALTHOUGH printing was not invented in Holland, the nation would not have been unworthy of that honour, for there is a widespread culture of the book among all classes of the population, and the newspaper and periodical press makes further a very large contribution to its intellectual food. Nearly two thousand booksellers and publishers are engaged in the task of bringing within easy reach of their customers everything they wish to read. It is no unusual thing to find a decently equipped retail bookshop in quite unimportant townlets, and even in villages. By an admirable arrangement every publisher sends parcels of books for the various retailers all over the country to one central house in Amsterdam — *het Bestelhuis voor den Boekhandel* (the Booksellers' Collecting and Distributing Office). In this establishment the publishers' parcels are opened, and all books sent by the various publishers for one retailer are packed together and forwarded to him, by rail, steamer, or other cheap mode of conveyance. In consequence, any doctor, clergyman, or schoolmaster can receive a penny or twopenny pamphlet in his out-of-the-way home, as well as any book or periodical from London, Paris, Berlin, Vienna, etc., within a remarkably short time, without trouble, and without extra expense in postage, by simply applying to the local bookseller.

The Dutch are very cosmopolitan in their reading. Many children of the superior working classes learn French at the primary schools; most children of the middle class pick up English and German as well at the secondary schools, and a large proportion of them are able to talk in these three foreign languages; and as opportunities for intercourse are not over-abundant in the smaller towns, they keep up their knowledge of these languages by reading. Indeed, the five millions of Dutchmen are, relatively, the largest buyers of foreign literature in Europe. The translator, however, comes to the rescue of those who succeed in forgetting so much of their foreign languages that they find reading them a very mitigated enjoyment. This question of translation is rather a sore point in the relations between Dutch and foreign authors and publishers. The pecuniary injury done to foreign authors, however, is very slight, while in reputation they have benefited; for if Dutch private libraries are not without their Shakespeare, Motley, Macaulay, Dickens, Thackeray, Kingsley, Browning, not to mention French and German classics, this is mainly due to the fact that the parents of the present generation had the opportunity of buying Dutch translations, and explained to their children the value and the beauty of these works.

Moreover, most authors and publishers in foreign countries, using languages with world-wide circulation, are apt to miscalculate the profits made by Dutch publishers, with their very limited market and limited sale. A royalty of £5 for the right of translating some novel would be regarded as a contemptibly small sum in the English book world, but £5 in Dutch currency presses heavily on the budget of a Dutch translation, of which only some hundred or so copies can be sold at a retail price of not quite five shillings, and is an almost prohibitive price to pay for the copyright of a novel which is only used as a *feuilleton* of a local paper with an edition of under a thousand copies a week. As a fact, many Dutch publishers pay royalties to their foreign colleagues as soon as the publication is important enough to bear the expense; but the majority clearly will only give up their ancient "right" of free translation, and agree to join the Berne Convention, if a practicable way can be found out of the financial difficulty. For the present, then, the Dutch are cosmopolitan readers, direct or indirect.

In the average bookseller's shop one finds, of course, a majority of novels — novels of all sorts and conditions—supplemented by literary essays and poems. In a number of cases the bookseller is not merely a shopkeeper who deals in printed matter, and supplies just what his customers ask for, but a man of education and judgment, who is well able to give his opinion on books and authors. Often he has read them, though oftener, of course, he is guided by the leading monthly and weekly magazines and reviews, and by the publishers' columns of the leading daily newspapers. The bookseller is thus in many cases the trusted manager and guiding spirit of one or more *Leesgezelschappen*, or "Reading Societies." These societies have a history. At the end of the eighteenth century they were often political and even revolutionary bodies. The members or subscribers met to discuss books, pamphlets, and periodicals, but frequently they discussed by preference the passages in the books bearing upon political conditions, and argued improvements which they considered desirable or necessary. As time passed by, and free institutions became the possession of the Dutch, the political mission of the Reading Society became exhausted, but the institution itself survived, and continues to the present day.

The *Leesgezelschap* owes its special form to another peculiarity of the Dutch — their intensely domesticated, home-loving character. Family life, with its fine and delicate intimacies between husband and wife, between parent and children, is the most attractive feature of national existence in the Netherlands. Family life is, indeed, the centre from which the national virtues emanate, because there the individual members educate each other in the practice of personal virtues. The Dutchman is not constitutionally reserved and shy; he knows how to live a full, strong, public life; he never shrinks from civic duties and social intercourse; but his love of home life takes the first place after his passion for liberty and independence. Club life in Holland is insignificant, and few clubs even attempt to create a substitute for home life; they are merely used for friendly intercourse for an hour or so every day, and as better-class restaurants. A Dutchman prefers to do his reading at home, in the domestic circle, with the members of his family, or in his study if he follows some scientific occupation, and his *Leesgezelschap* affords him the opportunity of doing this. There are military, theological, educational, philological, and all sorts of scientific reading societies, besides those for general literature. They work on the co-operative system. The manager is in many cases a local bookseller, buying Dutch and foreign books, magazines, reviews, illustrated weeklies and pamphlets in one or more copies, according to the number, the tastes, and the wants of the members. Most societies take in books and periodicals in four languages — Dutch, French, German, English — and so their members keep themselves well acquainted with the world's opinion. And all this, be it added, costs the subscriber vastly less than the fees of English circulating libraries, with their restricted advantages and heavy expenses of delivery.

Between the book and the newspaper lies a form of literature which is specifically Dutch—the *Vlugschrift*, *brochure*, or pamphlet. The *brochure* is an old historical institution. In the eighteenth century it was very popular as a vehicle for the zeal of fiery reformers, who thus vented their opinions on burning political questions of the day. There is no necessity nowadays for these small booklets, so easily hidden from suspicious eyes, though the *brochure* is still used whenever, in stirring speech or impassioned sermon, Holland's leading men address themselves to the emotions of the hour. These *brochures*, as a rule, cost no more than sixpence, yet, none the less, the thrifty Dutch have *Leesgezelschappen* which buy and circulate them among their subscribers; they take everything from everybody, never caring whose opinions they read upon the various subjects of current interest, a trait which evidences a very praiseworthy lack of bias.

This lack of bias is not so obvious so far as newspaper reading is concerned. Like other people, the Dutch take such newspapers as defend or represent their own political opinions, and often affect towards journals on the other side a contemptuous indifference which is only half real.

The Dutch as Readers

Political parties in Holland differ slightly from those of Great Britain, except that in the former country politics and religion go together. Thus in Holland a Liberal who at the same time is not advanced in religious thought hardly exists, and would scarcely be trusted. In consequence the Liberals were not defeated at the last general elections because they were Liberals, but because their opponents (the Anti-Revolutionists and Roman Catholics) denounced them as irreligious and atheistical. In political strife the religious controversy takes the form of an argument for and against the influence of religious dogma upon politics and education.

Now, as far as journalism goes, the Liberal and Radical newspapers unquestionably take the lead. The Roman Catholics are like the Anti-Revolutionists, very anxious to provide their readers with wholesome news, but this anxiety is not successfully backed up by care that this wholesome news shall be early as well; hence their journalism is somewhat behind the times. Of most of the progressive newspapers it may be said that the whole of the contents are interesting; as to the rest, they are only interesting because of the leading articles, which are sometimes written by eminent men.

As far as circulation goes, *Het Nieuws van den Dag* can boast to be the leading journal, its edition running to nearly 40,000 copies a day. Up to the present its editors have been advanced, or "Modern," Protestant clergymen, in the persons of Simon Gorter, H. de Veer, and P. H. Ritter. Although not taking a strong line in politics, its inclinations are decidedly towards moderate Liberalism, and, thanks to its cheap price,—14*s.* 6*d.* per annum,— its extensive, prudently, and carefully selected and worded supply of news, and its sagacious management, it became *the* family paper of the Dutch, excellently suiting the quiet taste of the middle class of the nation. It is found everywhere save in those few places where the Roman Catholic Church has sufficient influence to get it boycotted. The *Nieuws*, as it is generally called, gives from twenty-four to thirty-two, and even more, pages of closely printed matter, of which the advertisements occupy rather over than under half. One does not see it read in public more than any other Dutch paper, and two reasons account for this. One is the fact that, as has been said, a Dutchman prefers to do his reading at home—*met een boekje, in een hoekje* (with my book in a quiet corner) is the Dutchman's ideal of cosy literary enjoyment. Then, too, Dutch newspaper publishers prefer a system of safe quarterly subscriptions to the chance of selling one day a few thousand copies less than the other, since even the largest circulation in Holland is too limited for risky commercial vicissitudes. Hence they make the price for single numbers so high that only the prospect of long hours in a railway-carriage frightens a Dutchman into buying one or more newspapers.

The *Nieuwe Rotterdamsche Courant* is another typical Dutch newspaper, but appealing to quite other instincts than the *Nieuws*. In their quiet way the Dutch are rather proud of their *Nieuwe Rotterdammer*, which inspires something like awe for its undeniable, but slightly ponderous, virtues. The *Nieuwe Rotterdammer* is absolutely Liberal, and stands no Radical or Social Democratic nonsense ; its leading articles are lucid, cool, logical, and to the point ; it has correspondents everywhere, at home and abroad ; and all staunch Liberals of a clear-cut, even dogmatic type, who love Free Trade and look upon municipal and State intervention as pernicious, swear by it. The present chief editor is Dr. Zaayer, formerly a Liberal member of the Second Chamber of the States-General, a shrewd, well-read Dutchman, with a splendid University education ; and the manager, J. C. Nijgh, is as clever a man of business as Rotterdam can produce. As far as it is possible to lead Dutchmen by printed matter, the *Nieuwe Rotterdammer* does it. Its supply of news is so fresh and so reliable that everybody reads it, even the Roman Catholics in North Brabant and Limburg, Holland's two Catholic counties.

The next important newspaper is *Het Algemeen Handelsblad* of Amsterdam, which is peculiarly the journal of the Amsterdam merchants, shipowners, and traders. The *Handelsblad* is not so exclusively Liberal as its competitor in Rotterdam, for its inclinations are of a more advanced turn, and it is always ready to admit rather Radical articles on social matters if written by serious men. Its chief editor is Dr. A. Polak, of whom it is said that what he does not know about the working and meaning of the Dutch constitution and the Dutch law is hardly worth knowing. His articles display a calm, sound, scientific brain and an honest, straightforward mind. Its managing editor is Charles Boissevain, whose contributions to the paper, entitled *Van Dag tot Dag* (From Day to Day) are equally admirable for brilliancy of style, broadness of spirit, and the manly outspokenness of their contents. This journal has likewise an extensive staff and a huge army of correspondents at home and abroad.

A third Liberal journal of growing influence is the Radical *Vaderland*, of which the late Minister of the Interior, Mr. H. Goeman Borgesius, now a member of the Second Chamber, was chief editor during many years, though there no longer exists any personal connection between the two, and the *Vaderland* is, if anything, more advanced in politics than its former editor. Its chief influence is at The Hague, formerly a stronghold of Conservatism, until the Conservative party disappeared entirely.

Other Liberal, Radical, and Social Democratic newspapers are published all over the country, the most important and influential being the Liberal-Democratic *Arnhemsche Courant*.

Mr. Troelstra, one of the Socialist leaders, edits a daily, *Het Volk* (The People), a well-written party newspaper, whose influence, however, does not extend beyond its party.

Professor Abraham Kuyper, leader of the Anti-Revolutionist or Calvinist party, the largest but one in the country, was editor of the *Standaard* until he became President Minister of the Netherlands. In opposition to the Liberal principle, as formulated by the Italian Cavour, " A Free Church in a Free State," he maintains that the Bible, being God's Word, is the only possible basis for any State, and holds that the King and the Government derive their power and authority not from the people, but from God. His *Standaard* is another proof that whatever this universal genius does bears the unmistakable stamp of his power and personality. One may be thoroughly opposed to his principles, but nobody can help admiring the sterling merit of his leading articles. If Kuyper writes or speaks upon any subject under the sun, you will be sure to find him thoroughly acquainted with it ; but then his turn of mind is so original and his style is so brilliant, that he discloses points of view which give it fresh interest to those who most cordially disagree with him. The brilliancy of his journalistic powers is not confined, however, to his leaders.

The *Standaard* has another and more purely

polemical feature, its *Driestars* — short paragraphs, separated in the column by three asterisks, whence their name. These *Driestars* are the pride and the wonder of the Dutch Press, on account of their trenchant, clever, courageous wording, a wording which is sure to incite the opponent to bitter defence or fiery attack, and to provide the adherent with an argument so finely sharpened and polished that he delights in the possession of so excellent a weapon.

Dr. Kuyper's political opponent in the Calvinist party is Mr. A. F. de Savornin Lohman, the leader of the aristocrats, whereas Kuyper is the head of the *kleine luyden*—the humble toilers of the fields and towns. Mr. Lohman was a member of the first Calvino-Catholic Cabinet, and is still a great power in his party; in consequence his *Nederlander* exerts some influence, though not nearly so much as the *Standaard*.

The two most prominent Roman Catholic newspapers are the Conservative *Tyd* (Time) and the somewhat Democratic *Centrum*. Both are party papers pure and simple, and are excellently edited, so far as party politics are concerned, by clever, well-educated, well-read men. The *Centrum* frequently enjoys the co-operation of Dr. Herman Schaepman, the priest-poet, whose somewhat ponderous eloquence is agreeably relieved by a glowing enthusiasm and a refreshing force of conviction.

Kuyper, Boissevain, and Schaepman are, indeed,

The Dutch as Readers

three journalists of whom any country might be proud. Their style, their individuality, and their mental power are equally remarkable, and though living and working in different grooves of life, using different modes of thought, and cherishing different ideals, they powerfully impress and influence their readers by the purity of their aims, the honesty of their convictions, and the chivalry of their controversial methods. But of the three Boissevain is the only one who is a journalist for the sake of journalism. Yet neither Calvinist nor Catholic journal tries to compete with the *Nieuwe Rotterdammer* or the *Handelsblad* in the publication of original and high-class information. They aim rather at providing their readers with the necessary party arguments, and the news is a matter of secondary importance.

As to the provinces in general, of the 1300 towns and villages of Holland, nearly 300 are the happy possessors of a local newspaper of some description, and altogether 1700 daily and weekly journals, devoted variously to the representation of political, clerical, mercantile, scientific, and other interests, are published in the whole country.

The Dutch like to see more than one newspaper, but the majority of people cannot afford to be dual subscribers, and a great many cannot even afford to buy a single news-sheet regularly. Hence agencies exist for circulating the papers from one reader to another. Those who receive them straight from the publisher pay most, and those who are contented to enjoy their news when one, two, or three days old pay but a small fee. The newspaper circulating agency is very general in Holland, and in centres of restricted domestic resources it plays a very useful place in social and political life.

CHAPTER XVII

POLITICAL LIFE AND THOUGHT

HOLLAND is a democratic kingdom. Democracy was born there in the sixteenth century, and is still unquestionably thriving. But democracy was born in peculiar circumstances; it was reared by men whose ideas of democracy differed, for, while the leaders of the nation consistently worked for popular government, they did not all or always mean exactly the same thing by the word "people," and hence did not aim at exactly the same goal. The French Revolution of the eighteenth century upset the outward form of the Dutch Commonwealth; it did away with ancient and more or less obsolete fetters, which proved no longer strong enough to support the growth of political life, though still sufficiently strong to hinder it. It could do nothing for, and add nothing to, the profound love of liberty and the passion for independence which are dearer to every Dutchman than life itself, but it could and did extend the blessing of political and religious freedom to a greater number of people. Love of liberty brought about the disestablishment of the Church, and love of toleration made Holland follow this measure in the fifties by the emancipation of the Roman Catholics.

Everyone who is acquainted with Dutch history understands that these two things have as much meaning for Dutch political as for Dutch religious life. But side by side with religious and political freedom came also economic freedom. The guilds were abolished, and so the bonds by which the handicrafts had been prevented from moving with the movements of the times, and thus of living a healthy life, were swept away. The social revolution acted like the doctor who enters a close and stuffy sick room and throws open the windows and door, so that the invalid may get the very first necessity of life—fresh air. So it was with a sigh of relief that the Dutch— and not they alone—said, " No State interference in matters of trade and industry; let us keep open the windows and doors ! "

No doctor, however, will compel his patient to live in a constant draught, winter and summer, since upon one occasion a liberal admission of fresh air was necessary to save that patient's life. There can be no doubt that during the nineteenth century the doors and windows were kept open rather too long. The great employers of labour were strong enough to stand the draught, for centuries of prosperity had made them a powerful class; but their men had no such advantages, and they were worse off when steam-power brought about another revolution by creating the so-called system of "capitalistic production" and the growth of the large industries. Hence it comes about that Holland, like all civilised countries, is now trying to find out how far the windows and the doors must be closed, so as to allow the men to live as well as the masters. This, in few words, characterises Dutch party politics from the social and economic side.

Political parties in the Netherlands obviously differ not only in their views upon political, religious, and economic issues, but also as to the degree of precedence to be allowed to each of these three departments of national life and thought. The Liberals say, "Politics first; if these are sound and religion and commerce are free, everything will be right." The Social Democrats reply, "Politics only concern us as a means of obtaining real and substantial economic liberty and material equality; religion does not affect us at all, and certainly does not help to solve the practical problems of human life." Differing from both, the Anti-Revolutionists assert, "Whosoever leaves the firm ground of God's Word, the Holy Scriptures, as the only true basis for public and private action, can have neither sound politics nor sound economics." The Roman Catholics also put religion on the first plane, but they are in the most difficult position of all. They are a minority, even a decreasing minority, and know perfectly well that they will never be a majority ; so they recognise that in the first place they must try to be good Dutchmen, faithful, loyal citizens of the State, while in the second place they must not give up one single ideal of their Church. Their faith in the eternal existence of their ecclesiastic system enables them on the one hand to be patient and to wait, just as on the other hand it teaches them not to sit still, but to act, to work, either by themselves or conjointly with any party that may assist them to realise, or even to get nearer to, any of their religious ideals.

When the Liberals, in the middle of the nineteenth century, did an act of great toleration by emancipating the Roman Catholic Church, the Protestants threw over the Liberal Cabinet, and the Liberal leader, Thorbecke, was returned to Parliament by the most Catholic town of Holland, Maestricht, in Limburg. But afterwards the Anti-Revolutionists raised the cry for denominational education, and the Dutch Liberals were rather sore to find that their former friends joined their antagonists. The soreness was in consequence of a miscalculation; the Liberals had forgotten that in becoming emancipated the Roman Catholics did not become Liberals, but remained Roman Catholics as before, faithful to their creed, and to their ideals, even at the cost of political friendship.

The common ground upon which Anti-Revolutionists and Roman Catholics meet is the

PARLIAMENT HOUSE AT THE HAGUE. VIEW FROM THE GREAT LAKE

conviction that religion must in everything be the starting-point. The Anti-Revolutionists take the Scriptures as such; the Roman Catholics accept the Pope's decisions, given *ex cathedrâ*, as inspired by the Holy Spirit and transmitted to him by Conclaves and Councils. For the rest, Rome's creed is sheer idolatry to the Anti-Revolutionist Protestants, whereas Rome looks upon all Protestants as lost heretics. But both, again, consider such Protestants—the so-called "Moderns"—who reject the Trinity, the miracles, the Divine origin of the Bible, and certain other dogmas, as simple atheists, and as most "Moderns" are Liberals, and *vice-versâ*, they proclaim the Liberal State to be an atheistic State.

Strictly speaking, there is really no Conservative party in Holland, for it ceased to exist in the beginning of the seventies. After Thorbecke gave Holland the Liberal constitution of 1848, the Conservatives tried for a time to obstruct the country's political development, but ultimately they gave up the attempt, and their best and ablest men, Mr. J. Heemsherk Azn and Earl C. Th. van Lynden van Sandenburg, headed Liberal Cabinets as men professing very moderately progressive views, yet openly opposed to the restoration of the somewhat autocratic and aristocratic conditions which prevailed before 1848, in consequence of the reaction against the chaotic era of the French Revolution and Napoleon Bonaparte. Yet though there is no Conservative party in Holland, there are, none the less, Conservatives in every party.

The Liberal party counts three sections, the Old Liberals, the Radico-Liberals, and the Liberal Democrats. The Old Liberals adhere to Thorbecke's principles, and maintain that it is the primary business of a Liberal State to promote individuality and to create on this basis the general conditions by which social development can be achieved. According to them the State has no right to interfere in everything, to cure everything, to provide everything, as the collectivist would like; on the contrary, its first duty is abstinence—simply to preserve a fair field and to show no favour. These Old Liberals, in fact, regard the State as a legal corporation which exists merely to administer justice and to guard the constitutional rights of its citizens.

Their political friends and next-of-kin are the Radico-Liberals of the "Liberal Union," who form, for the present, the bulk of the party. They admit the value of individual energy and enterprise, and hold that unlimited scope must be allowed to these; they even contend that, on the whole, the system of unfettered individualism proved to be more in the workman's favour than the opposite; but they also admit that this condition is not such as it might and ought to be, and in consequence they do not object to social legislation wherever individual efforts fail.

The advanced Liberal Democrats (*de Vryzin-*

Political Life and Thought

nige Democraten) differ fundamentally from both the foregoing parties. They give prominence to political rights and franchises, and hence fall foul of a leading clause (Clause 80) of the Constitution, which confers electoral powers upon only such adult male inhabitants as "possess characteristics of capability and prosperity." The members of the "Liberal Union" admit that the requirement of a certain measure of prosperity withholds from numbers of citizens the right to influence their country's affairs by their votes. They admit also that the Constitution ought to be altered on this point, but they doubt whether it is sound practical politics to put this item in the foreground. They say, in effect, "We can quite well provide the country with adequate social legislation either with or without the help of the disfranchised section of the population, for if we propose measures dealing with social problems, even the more conservative amongst us will not object, and those measures will come on the statute-book. But there is not the slightest chance that we shall ever get the Old Liberals to give the franchise to poor and destitute people who have no financial stake whatever in the country. So by insisting upon adult suffrage you merely postpone social legislation indefinitely. Moreover, the object of our social legislation can only be to make the poorer class more capable and more prosperous, and as soon as that end is gained they get the franchise automatically, without any change of the Constitution." To this the Liberal Democrats reply : " Social legislation must not be regarded as a grudgingly admitted necessity, it is the paramount duty of the State; and as social legislation principally affects those who are now disfranchised, it is only just to begin by affording them the opportunity of expressing their opinions upon the subject, and hence to alter the Constitution so as to give them votes, for they know best what they want."

The Liberal Democrats deny, in fact, that the State can make any laws that do not affect the social life as well as the legal position of its citizens, and contend that those who hold that natural laws rule the social relations of man with man, and that on this ground the State ought to refrain from interference, merely allow the State to protect the stronger against the weaker classes, whereas its duty is the contrary. Positive interference in social matters is, according to them, the State's duty, and it may only refrain when the free operation of social forces creates no conditions or relationships which offend modern ideas of justice and equity.

The Democrats have, unquestionably, by their secession, greatly crippled the strength of the Liberal party, and it will be long before the younger generation of Liberals can take the places thus vacated and a rejuvenated and unanimous party can issue from the present dissensions.

Political Life and Thought

The only other political party in Holland who do not accept religion as the one safe starting-point for politics are the Social Democrats. When the German Socialists of the school of Marx discovered how the sudden development of steam and machinery was followed by a vast amount of distress amongst the labouring classes, affecting also such of the lower middle class as principally traded with workpeople, they at once jumped at the conclusion that the same thing was bound to go on forever. Perhaps it was with a feeling of despair, therefore, that the father of Dutch Social Democracy, F. Domela Nieuwenhuys, gradually drifted into anarchism, or, as he prefers to call it, Free Socialism, and finally abandoned all political action. The younger generation, led by F. van der Goes, H. van Kol, and, last but not least, P. J. Troelstra, still vigorously carry on the fray, however, and a very considerable number of Dutch workmen follow them. Their ambition is to conquer political power in Holland, and as soon as they have it to revolutionise, not the country, but the statute-book, in such a manner that they may acquire the economic power as well. Of course, they wish to abolish individual property in all the means of production, and to make the State the owner of all these; and it is their hope that a general love for the commonwealth, and zeal for the general welfare of all, may take the place of the present egotism and sordid pursuit of wealth.

The Anti-Revolutionists also have their Conservatives and Progressives. Dr. Kuyper always speaks of a " Left " and a " Right " wing of his party, and as the Conservative " Right " is largely composed of the members of the Dutch nobility, he once sneeringly called this faction " the men with the double names." Their proper title is " Free Anti-Revolutionists," and their leader, Jhr. A. F. de Savornin Lohman, who in 1888, with Baron Ae. Mackay (Lord Reay's cousin), led the first Anti-Revolutionist-Catholic majority in the Second Chamber of the States-General.

The third faction is headed by Dr. Bronsveld, and is called the " Christian Historicals," who differ on one great principle from the two others, inasmuch as they seek the re-establishment of the Netherlands Hervormde Kerk as State Church.

But, however much they differ in practical measures, their common ground is the recognition of the Holy Scriptures as the only right basis for statesmanship, and their conviction that the present modern State is merely a passing, non-Dutch consequence of the French Revolution and its disastrous teachings. They all agree that the Netherlands should be governed according to the principles that made Holland great and powerful ever since the Reformation of the sixteenth century. Dr. Kuyper is fully convinced that the French Revolution thrust Holland off its historical line of development, and he wants to return, as near as possible, to the point reached before that event, or, at any rate, to lead the State forward in the old direction.

All Anti-Revolutionists hold that their first civic duty is obedience to God;—if conscience requires resistance to the authorities, resist them, whatever you may suffer. At the same time they eschew clericalism and object to every form of State Church. Hence one of their chief antipathies is Clause 171 of the Constitution, which continues in the same way as before the disestablishment of the Church the payments by the Exchequer to various clergymen of all denominations. In opposition to this they demand entire and absolute liberty and equality for all churches and confessions, and, theoretically, admit that one can be a member of their party without being of their creed. With regard to education, they do not desire to substitute denominational State schools for the present neutral ones, but they object that at present the State compels parents, who desire religious schools for their children, not only to find all necessary money for these "free schools," but to contribute in addition to the school taxes, to the advantage of such parents as hold that secular and religious education are better disconnected, since religious education must needs be dogmatical and sectarian, and that the churches and not the State should look to this, whereas school education can quite well be given without reference to religion at all.

The Anti-Revolutionist position, on the other hand, is that it is not the State's duty to provide school or any other education, all education being a matter of private concern for the individual family, and not a public business at all ; though they allow that where parents are unable to maintain them, schools may be erected by the taxpayers' money. They also deprecate legislation against intemperance, immorality, and prostitution, because they think such laws do not remove the evils themselves, but merely attack their visible signs and relieve moral trespassers of part of their responsibility by protecting them against certain consequences of their acts. They are opposed to the legal and compulsory observance of the Sabbath, holding this to be an affair of the churches and of individuals ; but they support laws to compel employers to allow their men a sufficient weekly rest on Sundays. They admit a limited State interference in social matters, but contend that it must not discourage individual effort, or create a host of officials, inspectors, and controllers. The franchise must, according to them, never enable one section of the nation to supersede the other by sheer force of numbers ; they do not admit that the majority system is the ultimate and only criterion of legality and justice ; moreover, the family being the unit from which the commonwealth has grown into existence, they contend that heads of families are the natural electors. Where the Old Liberals say that the financial

Political Life and Thought

test is the right one for voters, the Anti-Revolutionists hold that no one has a real stake in the country who has not a family and knows nothing of the responsibilities involved thereby. Dr. Kuyper is the democratic leader of what he calls, in classical but antiquated Dutch, the *Kleine luyden* (the "Little people") amongst the Anti-Revolutionists. He knows that the "double-named" Free Anti-Revolutionists have little sympathy with his social programme, but this does not matter, since they are perfectly well aware of the fact that they owe everything, as far as political power goes, to the "Little people."

Finally, there is the Left Wing of the Roman Catholic party, who derive their social convictions from Pope Leo's Encyclica, *Rerum Novarum*, which affords a great many points upon which joint action is possible, for Leo XIII. is often called in Holland "the Workmen's Pope." Both Anti-Revolutionists and Roman Catholics entertain entirely different political ideals, but they agree upon this, that the modern Liberal State is not really neutral in religious matters, but is "Modern" Protestant, and "Modern" Protestantism spells atheism in their eyes; and both regard a weak and fragile Christian as a better citizen than the best atheist or agnostic. For this reason they are combined in hostility to the existing system of elementary education, which they suspect of an atheistic tendency. These two questions, religion and the schools, virtually exhaust the vital points of agreement between the Anti-Revolutionists and the Roman Catholics, though in an emergency they might possibly unite on social legislation or some mild form of Protection. The latter would, however, have to be very mild indeed, for Dr. Kuyper is a Free Trader, and the "Little people" like cheap bread just as well as other folk. For Holland it might be a matter of great importance if progressive social legislation became Kuyper's chief work.

There is no doubt a great drawback in this mixing up by all parties of politics and religion. Kuyper, the Calvinist; Schaepman, the Catholic; Drucker, Treub, and Molengraaf, the Liberal Democrats; Goeman Borgesius, the man of the "Liberal Union"; and Troelstra, the Socialist, all have many common ideas on social questions, although they may differ in principles and seek different aims. Each of them, however, has Conservative opponents in his own party, and there is just a possibility that the next few years may bring about not only a healthy measure of social development, but also a much-desired readjustment of parties on non-theological, undogmatical lines.

CHAPTER XVIII

THE ADMINISTRATION OF JUSTICE

THERE are two very marked differences between the administration of justice in Holland and in England. The first is, that what are called "petty offences" are not tried and disposed of summarily in the former country. There the offender in such cases is subjected to a process known as "verbalisation"—that is, his name, address, age, and all particulars of the offence are noted by the police; and he is thereupon informed that he will be called upon to give an account of himself later. A week or two may pass before the offender receives verbal or printed notice requiring his presence before the Court of the Cantonal Judge, which answers somewhat to the English Police Court. This delay in the administration of justice is regarded as a great defect even in Holland, and one which is more and more being recognised. The establishment of the Police Court as known and conducted in England is felt, therefore, to be a great *desideratum*, and it is by no means unlikely that it may be introduced before long, since the Dutch have always shown themselves ready to adopt any modification of their own institutions which the experience of other countries may prove to be clearly desirable.

The second difference is that trial by jury as Englishmen understand it does not exist in the Netherlands. But here the Dutch are not likely to abandon their own tradition. The jury in Holland is composed of experienced and qualified judges, who are not apt to modify their opinions as to the guilt or innocence of accused persons owing to the tears of the latter or the passionate appeals of their advocates. Rightly or wrongly, the most eminent lawyers in Holland ascribe the often-recurring cases of miscarriage of justice in some countries which have adopted the jury system to this system itself, and it is very improbable, therefore, that in this respect the Dutch will copy any of their neighbours.

The organisation of justice in Holland originated in the Code Napoleon, which was introduced shortly after the country's annexation to the French Empire. In the judicial system in vogue to-day, which is the result of modifications introduced at various times during the last century, and particularly by a law of the year 1895, the administration of justice is vested in the High Court (*Hooge Raad*), the Provincial Courts of Justice (*Gerechtshoven*), the Arrondissements (*Rechtbanken*), and the Cantonal Courts (*Kantongerechten*).

The High Court consists of a President, a Vice-

President, from twelve to fourteen Councillors, a Procurator-General, three Advocates-General (who form, with the Procurator-General, the "Public Ministry" or Office of Public Prosecution), also a Greffier, or Clerk of Court, and two deputy Greffiers. Most of the appointments are made by the Sovereign, and are for life. The High Court is situated at The Hague, and its principal duty is to control the administration of justice by the lower Courts, a process known as "cassation." If, for example, one of the lower Courts has pronounced a sentence from which there is no appeal in that Court, and one of the contending parties is of opinion that the sentence is excessive, that party may require the High Court to cancel or annul (*casseer*) the verdict. When an appeal for cassation or annulment is thus made, the High Court has not to go into the question of the guilt or innocence of the contending parties, but merely into the question whether the lower Court has judged rightly or whether it was competent to judge the case at all. Such "cassations" occur almost daily, not because the High Court has a reputation for reversing the verdicts given below, but because the process offers at least a good chance of getting a sentence reduced. The Public Prosecution, however, has power to set in motion the process of cassation without being called upon so to do if the interests of justice should in its opinion require it. To the jurisdiction of the High Court belong also piracy cases, the apportionment of prizes made in war, and the determination of accusations against State officials of abuse of power.

Of Provincial Courts there are five, each composed of officials similar in name, though not in rank, to those of the High Court, and they, too, are for the most part appointed by the Crown, though not all for life. These Provincial Courts pronounce judgment in the second instance—that is, when the decision of a lower Court has been appealed against. This is, in fact, their principal function, though they also pronounce judgment in the first instance in cases of difference between the Cantonal Courts or Arrondissement Courts. The latter are so named from the divisions into which the country was split up for administrative purposes during the Napoleonic *régime*, for the existing arrondissement boundaries are virtually the same as those of ninety years ago.

There are twenty-three Arrondissement Courts, thirteen of the first-class and ten of the second-class. Their principal business is to pronounce judgment in the first instance, even in criminal cases, but they also decide in the final instance in cases of dispute between the Cantonal Courts, which are under their jurisdiction. They likewise adjudicate upon claims for compensation up to a certain amount, upon disputes regarding the boundaries of land and property, and upon complaints relating to water-supply, drainage, and the like, while cases of mendicancy, vagrancy, and evasion of taxes are decided by these Courts summarily.

The Cantonal Courts are, as already stated, the nearest equivalent in Holland to the English Police Courts. Their members, however, are legally trained and salaried men, though attached to each Court are several unsalaried deputies. The Judges of these Courts are appointed for life by the Crown, and the minor officials for a term of years. All the petty cases which in England come before the Police Court are in Holland adjudicated upon by the Cantonal Courts. Poaching, personal violence, cruelty to animals, damage done to dwellings, trees, or crops, are all cases for these Courts, and so long as the fines imposed do not exceed two guineas, their judgment is final, but in other cases the right of appeal exists.

Mention has just been made of the fact that even from the lowest Court of Law in Holland the amateur judge is rigidly excluded. No one who has not acquired the diploma of Doctor of Laws from one of the Dutch Universities is allowed to assume any responsible duty associated with the administration of justice. The same severe requirement is imposed upon the legal profession in general. The possession of the diploma of Doctor of Laws and Letters alone entitles a man to practise as advocate. Amongst themselves the members of the legal profession also exercise a sort of mutual surveillance by means of their Councils of Supervision and Discipline, whose duty it is to take care that nothing is done by an advocate which is contrary to the law or to the honour of the faculty. These Councils are chosen from amongst the lawyers themselves in all towns where there are more than fourteen resident advocates, but in smaller places their duties are discharged by the Provincial or Arrondissement Courts. Should a lawyer be guilty of any serious misdemeanour he is promptly expelled from the Community of Advocates, and he may be even refused the right to plead in any of the public Courts. In passing, it is an interesting feature of the Dutch judicial system that in every place where there is a Court of Justice, higher or lower, there exists a Consultation Bureau where people without means may obtain gratuitous advice in legal matters. Unless a charge laid before this Consultation Bureau appears on the face of it to be unsustainable, the Bureau appoints one of its members to act as legal adviser and counsellor to the applicant free of cost. In criminal cases the President of the Court concerned appoints a legal adviser for the accused, though the latter may choose another advocate if he pleases.

It will be interesting to enter one of these Dutch Courts of Law, and a Cantonal Court may perhaps best serve as an example, since that resembles most closely the English *forum* of the people—the Police Court. Let us assume that we are privileged persons, though engaged in

The Administration of Justice

serious legal business. We are bidden to make an appearance at a quarter to eleven o'clock in the morning, and, presenting ourselves at that hour, we take our seats on comfortable chairs, ranged round a long square table in the large public waiting-room. As many other people are coming in, and the room threatens soon to be crowded, a considerate attendant, knowing that we are in favour with the grave and reverend seigniors who preside over the Court, shows us into another and smaller room, where one of the deputy Clerks (Greffier) is seated working at his books. One by one other persons come in, pay small sums of money, of which the deputy Clerk evidently keeps an exact account, together with the names and addresses of the payers, the amounts yet remaining due—everything, in fact, relating to each person's case. We note that some of the payers inquire how much they yet owe, and the sum being told them they forthwith take their departure. We learn that these are all people who were fined some time ago for petty offences, and who are, or pretend to be, unable to pay the full amount at once. Hence they are allowed to pay by instalments, and it is the duty of the Clerk to keep an accurate account of their contributions.

Our own turn having come round, we are now ushered into the Court, where we see His Worship the Judge seated at the head—which happens to be the middle—of a long table, covered by the inevitable green cloth. Papers, ink-stands, and pen are before him; at his left hand sits the Clerk, and next to him the first deputy Clerk. We observe, too, how carefully the proprieties are observed in the matter of dress. All the judicial functionaries present wear a costume consisting of a black toga reaching to the heels, with a white *bef*, or collar-band, hanging in front half-way down to the waist and also a black *barrette*, or square cap, as in France.

Five persons are seated in the chairs next to ours and opposite to the Judge. They have just testified that the last will of their parent has been duly carried out, and that each of them has received his share, being in this case " 3887 guilders, 7½ cents " (don't forget the half-cent, for attention to minutiæ is one of those characteristics of the Dutch which strikes us at every turn). Presently the Judge asks the eldest of the party whether his name is not " So-and-so." The answer being in the affirmative, His Worship nods to the Clerk, who begins to read out in clear and measured tones—

" I, So-and-so (description and address follow), hereby declare and testify to having received as my share in the heritage of my parent the sum legally apportioned to me, being 3887 guilders, 7½ cents."

Then the Judge asks: " Are you prepared to swear that this is true, and that as far as you know nothing is kept behind so that justice is not fully carried out?" This is the legal formula in use upon such an occasion, and it produces the expected reply. "Very well, then," proceeds the Judge, "repeat after me, ' So truly help me God Almighty!'" The familiar words of the Dutch oath are accompanied by the uplifting of the right hand and the pointing to Heaven of the first two fingers. Then follow the other four members of the family in order of age. All of them swear in the usual words except the second daughter, who demurs, on which the judicial eyebrows are raised in surprise. It appears that the maiden suffers from religious scruples, being firmly of opinion that swearing an oath is forbidden by Holy Scripture. The Judge listens respectfully, and simply answers, "Then repeat after me, ' I hereby solemnly declare that the words read out to me just now are the truth, the whole truth, and nothing but the truth.'" The conscientious witness having no objection to a simple affirmation, the words are promptly repeated, the business is completed, and the party are all allowed to withdraw. Now our own turn has come. One of our party, we will assume, has been appointed by the Cantonal Judge to be guardian over a minor son of another of our number. All declare who, what, and whence they are, and that the guardian has received his appointment with their common consent, while the guardian himself makes formal declaration of accepting the duty. He is thereupon sworn by the Judge in the occupation of his office, promising "to act in all things as a true and faithful guardian should act, so truly help me God Almighty." These several incidents are fairly typical of the sort of business which occupies the attention of these minor Courts. As we leave the building, however, we learn another piece of interesting information in the course of conversation with the deputy Clerk whose acquaintance we first made. It is that the principle of "punishment by instalments" is applied in the case of the poorer classes, not merely in the matter of fines, but also of imprisonment, save in criminal cases. Many a poor man, for instance, who shortly after being sentenced to, say, a week's or a fortnight's imprisonment has happened to find employment, would be ruined if compelled to go to prison at once. He is therefore allowed, as in Russia, to select his own time for surrendering himself to the prison authorities, and if, as often happens in poaching cases, two different offences have brought upon him two terms of imprisonment, he is allowed to come before the Judge, with the request that he may combine these two terms, beginning his incarceration at a fixed date. The Court to whose clemency he thus appeals generally grants the request, and the man is thus enabled to work for his livelihood whilst the demand for labour is general, and to go to prison when he happens to be out of work, and would only be one mouth more to feed at home, where

The Administration of Justice

his wife and children already find difficulty enough in making both ends meet. When imprisonment is thus postponed the offender receives from the Court a document on the presentation of which at the prison door the Master of the prison will admit him as a temporary occupant of one of the cells. Old gaol-birds, however, are not treated so tenderly, but the Judges soon learn by experience when and how to apply this merciful arrangement, and when to refuse it altogether.

In general the statistics of crime give Holland a decidedly favourable reputation. Serious misdemeanours are comparatively rare. Crimes like burglary, theft, and the like are certainly committed often enough, but there is no evidence to show that they are on the increase, while life and property are at least as secure in the large Dutch towns as anywhere else in Europe. The Hague, though a city of 220,000 inhabitants, is sufficiently protected by the comparatively small number of 220 policemen. Rotterdam and Amsterdam both have a larger number of policemen per thousand inhabitants than The Hague, but this is natural, owing to the more heterogeneous character of the population of these great commercial centres. It is a notable fact that in every town in Holland the Burgomaster or Mayor is the supreme head of the police, and that the Chief Commissary of Police must not merely co-operate with him but is in the last resort subject to his direct command.

In spite of the fact that Courts of summary

jurisdiction of the English type do not exist in Holland, the police authority possesses a considerable amount of power. Mention has been made of the process of "verbalisation" as applied to common misdemeanours. In the case of drunkenness or fighting, however, the offenders are at once taken before the Commissary of Police, who promptly deals with them. Offences against which the police are entirely powerless are those of adulteration of food, household quarrels so long as they remain within certain bounds, and an offence of quite modern origin known as "bottle-drawing" (*Anglicè*, "long-firm frauds"). This last is an ingenious species of fraud which has become very common in Holland of late years. A person orders a quantity of goods from merchants of various towns on the pretence of opening accounts, which he promises will quickly assume large dimensions. Consignment after consignment of wares is sent, but never paid for, and when at last the too trustful merchant discovers that he has been playing into the hands of a swindler he gets no redress, for the artful schemer has disappeared, taking with him the proceeds of the goods received. For a time this sort of fraud was quite popular, but then the eyes of the business community were opened, and the strong hand of the law fell upon several offenders with crushing weight, after which "bottle-drawing" lost in attractiveness. On the whole, the police in Holland are commendably energetic as well as dutiful, and the relationship between the police authority and the public is generally a friendly and trustful one.

It may be noted that the Dutch law strongly discourages divorce. In general the present generation is apt to regard separation and divorce with greater favour than its fathers did, but though this feeling may to some extent influence the decisions of Dutch Judges in divorce proceedings, the law itself, strictly interpreted, offers little hope to those who would weaken the marriage tie. When married people disagree to such an extent that a rupture between them is imminent, and a demand for divorce is made, proof is required that the demand comes only from one side, for divorce by common consent is against the law except in cases of adultery. In every other case the Judge of the Cantonal Court must do his utmost to effect a reconciliation. Should, however, a demand for divorce be repeated, this same Judge, or a Judge of a Superior Court, must again endeavour to bring the parties together, and only in the event of failure is judicial separation *a mensâ et thoro* pronounced, and this separation must exist for a number of years—as a rule seven—before actual divorce can take place. Nevertheless, both separation and divorce are far more frequent nowadays than ten or twenty years ago, owing largely to the judicial disposition to interpret the law more in accordance with what are known as "modern ideas."

Holland is one of the few countries which no longer tolerate capital punishment. It was abolished thirty years ago, and, in spite of the strenuous efforts of the reactionary party, it is not likely to be re-established. Quite recently, Mr. C. Loosjes wrote a pamphlet in advocacy of the re-enactment of capital punishment, and his position at the Ministry of Justice gave to this work considerable weight. His contention was that since capital punishment was abolished, the crimes of murder, attempted murder, poisoning, and parricide had increased, but Mr. Loosjes failed to make sufficient allowance for the fact that during the period covered by his statistics the population of the country had greatly increased. The fact is that during the twenty years preceding abolition considerably more crimes punishable by death occurred than during the twenty years following that act of clemency, civilization, and enlightenment, while as compared with other countries Holland takes a very favourable position indeed, standing, together with England, Belgium, and Germany, at the head of the nations having the smallest number of crimes of a kind usually punished by death.

CHAPTER XIX

RELIGIOUS LIFE AND THOUGHT

THE Dutch are a thoroughly religious people. Religious sentiments and introspective inclinations were bound to develop and prosper in the Low Lands, where vast plains of fertile land are only limited by the endless sea below, the unfathomable blue of heaven above; where man feels himself an atom, lost in the vastness of creation, yet safe, because he is placed there by the will of a beneficent Maker.

Introspective, personal, individualistic, self-centred are their painters and their poets. These were greatly so when Holland's fleets ruled the seas, and when Holland's influence and power were felt far beyond its own narrow frontiers; and they are still so in our days.

This individualism accounts for the many sects found among the Dutch Reformed. The Roman Catholic Church, the only episcopacy in Holland, numbers only two sections: those—the majority—who admit the infallibility of the Pope, and those—a small minority—who, although recognising the Pope as chief of the Church, do not agree with the decisions of the Vatican Council of 1870, proclaiming this papal infallibility. The Roman Catholic Church is a tolerably prospering institution, thanks to the absolute freedom which it, like all the sister Churches, enjoys in Holland, where, ever since the revolution of 1795, a State Church has been an unknown thing. On the whole, however, its growth is not keeping pace with the increase of the population. A former census indicated that the Roman Catholics numbered two-fifths of the whole population, but the latest puts them down at only one-third, and in the Second Chamber of the States-General there are only twenty-five Roman Catholic members out of a total of a hundred representatives. Their present organisation dates from 1853, when the Liberals agreed to the appointment by the Pope of one Archbishop in Utrecht, and four Bishops in Haarlem, Bois-le-Duc, Breda, and Roermond. The bishoprics are divided in decanates, and in 1858 the Pope completed the organisation by instituting chapters, each governed by one provost and eight canons. The Archbishops and Bishops do not officially participate in political life in Holland, although, as a matter of course, nobody can help noticing their influence upon the electorate; the minor clergy as a rule are less discreet in this matter than their chiefs, whereas the political leader of the Roman Catholics in the Second Chamber is Dr. Herman Schaepman, a priest, a professor at the Seminary of Rysenburg, a statesman, an orator, and a poet, whose quintuple attainments are equally admired, although his scientific importance is not generally considered to be quite as weighty as the rest of his remarkable personality.

Far more significant for Dutch religious life are the other two-thirds of the population, Protestants to the backbone. The former State Church, the Netherlands Reformed Church, was left in a most awkward position when, in 1795, disestablishment was forced upon it. Up till 1848, when Jan Rudolf Thorbecke saved Holland and the Royal House from another revolution, by imposing a Liberal constitution upon the reluctant King William II., the Netherlands Reformed Church had no sound, well-regulated status; but not before 1870 was the last tie connecting State and Church severed. The State now no longer exercises spiritual or other supervision, but merely pays a yearly allowance to the various clergymen without vindicating or claiming any rights in return.

On the other hand, the State no longer pays or appoints University professors to teach specific reformed theology; every Church of every description looks after this on behalf of its own students, and whereas the Roman Catholic clergy are educated at the Seminaries, the General Synod, the supreme governing board of the Netherlands Reformed Church, nominates two professors for each of the four Dutch Universities at Leyden, Utrecht, Groningen, and Amsterdam.

It is necessary to point here to a peculiarity in Dutch religious and political life. At the time when Liberal politics were developing in Holland, critical and historical research made itself conspicuous in the teaching of leading Dutch ecclesiastics like Scholten and Kuenen. The Reformation upset the Divine authority of the Pope; these modern critics denied and destroyed the faith in the Divine authority of the Bible. They were educated, and afterwards taught their lessons at the University of Leyden, where the future Liberal statesmen of Holland were preparing for their task; they had the same ideals, the same modes of thought.

The ecclesiastics called themselves "Moderns"; the politicians were designated "Liberals." Both vindicated the supreme right of freedom in everything: free criticism, free research, free thought, free speech. The reign of pure intellectualism became supreme; every emotion, every sentiment was dissected, measured by the measure of inexorable logic; and rationalism, later doomed to bankruptcy, was in those days all-triumphant.

So it came about that the Liberals were "Moderns" and the "Moderns" Liberals; and as the State was for a quarter of a century governed by Liberals who involuntarily made the Church "Modern," populated by Liberals, so it also came about that their religious opponents became their political foes.

These opponents were called "Orthodox";

INTERIOR OF THE CHURCH AT DELFTSHAVEN WHERE THE PILGRIM FATHERS WORSHIPPED BEFORE LEAVING FOR NEW ENGLAND

they felt this imposition of liberty as the worst coercion one man could apply to another—the coercion of the conscience. They did not care to see the Bible treated as a piece of sheer human manufacture, however exalted; they felt it a burning shame to have to pay taxes towards the maintenance of irreligious, or even anti-religious, scientific chairs and colleges. They thought of their stern forefathers, who had broken the power of the mighty Spanish Empire, strengthened by God's Word and by that only. To them the Netherlands Reformed Church and the Netherlands State lost their sound and only safe basis by the assertion that there was something changeable, something non-eternal in the Bible; that this Bible, revered as containing the Holy Scriptures, might be replaced by any human system of thought to serve as the foundation for the structure of the State.

This blending of Modernism and Liberalism afforded to them absolute proof that any abandonment of the ancient creed and the revered Confession meant ruin both to State and Church. So they followed the time-honoured practice of the Dutch race; they separated, broke away from a species of liberty which was not of their liking, and became "Anti-Revolutionists" and "Separatists" (*Afgescheidenen*); Calvin, with his staunch, severe Protestantism, being their ideal as statesman and spiritual leader.

The Dutch language has two words for one

thing: *Hervorming* and *Reformatie*. But there is a vast difference between the Netherlands *Hervormde* and the Netherlands *Gereformeerde* Churches. The former is the late State Church, the latter is the Church of the *Afgescheidenen*, who, before joining the Netherlands *Gereformeerde*, called themselves *Christelyk Gereformeerde*. These two joined in 1892, and are now known as the *Gereformeerde Kerken* (the Reformed Churches).

Their leader is Professor Abraham Kuyper, the present President Minister of the Netherlands. He, like Dr. Schaepman, is a born orator, a prolific author, a scientific ecclesiastic, a strong democratic leader of men, an admirable organiser, and perhaps the most brilliant journalist in Holland; but beyond this, he is a staunch Protestant of the strictest Calvinistic type, to whom the Roman Catholic Church is a blasphemous and idolatrous institution. In 1879, he created the "Society for Higher Education on a Reformed Basis," and in 1880 his "Free University" was consecrated in the "Nieuwe Kerk" (the New Church) at Amsterdam, Dr. Kuyper ever since the opening acting as one of the professors. His flock is now strong in numbers, but his and their faith is stronger and has worked miracles, building churches and schools, maintaining preachers and teachers, finding money for everything, and finally, for the second time, gaining a political victory, with the help of such strange auxiliaries as the Roman Catholics. What unites them is the conviction they have in common that a State and a Government not led themselves by religion must lead a nation to perdition. To them Liberal Governments, although theoretically free from clerical influence, are actually led and unduly influenced by the "Modern" Protestants of Holland. These "Modern" Protestants reject the dogma of the Holy Trinity and various other dogmas which the Roman Catholics and the Orthodox Protestants consider the essence of the Christian creed; they are, therefore, in the opinion of the latter, mere atheists, and consequently unfit to rule the destinies of a nation.

These "Modern" Protestants came to the fore during the last fifty years. The University of Groningen taught a humanism, which created a reaction towards the ancient confessors of the creed, the "Reveil," or awakening. Subsequently modern cosmosophy tried to adjust its opinions to modern science and the results of modern research in every branch of human knowledge. This was a great blow to the ancestral faith and the venerable Confession. In those days Coenraad Busken Huet published his *Letters on the Bible*, popularising the scientific criticisms of the Sacred Book. Gradually Leyden's University took the lead, Johannes Henricus Scholten, Abraham Kuenen, and the Utrecht philosopher Cornelis Willem Opzoomer assisting the new movement by their profound knowledge, their irresistible logic, their brilliant style, and their high enthusiasm. In those years Holland went through all the throes accompanying the appearance of new life; it was a time of intellectual stress and strain, a time of controversial storm in which unrelenting criticism and critical research carried away everything that could not exist in the light of exact science and exacter thinking.

Jacobus Izaäk Doedes, Johannes Jacobus van Oosterzee, Chantepie de la Saussaye, the successors of Guillaume Groen van Prinsterer, Jan Rudolf Thorbecke's greatest opponent, and Isaäc da Costa, Willem Bilderdyk's famous pupil, defended the ancient creed, but the General Synod was "Modern" and the "Orthodox" had a difficult time.

In numbers of places the "domines," or preachers, were Orthodox, and in order to provide their own followers with spiritual fare, the "Moderns" established in 1870 the *Nederlandsche Protestantenbond*, or Netherlands Protestant League. This League sees that all over the country "Modern" sermons are preached, "Modern" Sunday-schools instituted, meetings of Protestants arranged, and everything is done that can support or promote religious life.

Besides these two large bodies of Protestants, the Orthodox and the Moderns, Holland has a good many Lutherans, Baptists, or Mennonites, and Remonstrants. Of the Lutherans the most numerous are the Evangelical Lutherans, who faithfully maintain the Augsburg Confession, while the Moderns, known as Reinstated Lutherans, abandoned that organ of doctrine. There is not, however, much animosity between the two sects at the present time, neither making a strong point of dogma, but both giving a prominent place to the demands of Christian practice.

The Mennonites—so called after the Dutch reformer Menno Simons (1496–1561)—were in olden times the most persecuted Protestants of all. Roman Catholics, Lutherans, and Calvinists were equally hard upon them, and many of them lost their lives on account of their convictions. They have no test, no church, no rite, no clergy. They have fraternities, and in these the minister is the *voorganger* (guide or leader), though his education, social position, and general duties are the same as those of all other Protestant ministers. In Amsterdam they have their own Seminary, and the names of Professors Samuel Muller, Sytske Hoekstra Bzn, Jacob Gysbert de Hoop Scheffer, and Jan van Gilse are honoured in the country and outside the "General Baptist Society," as their central body is called. Their teaching and preaching appeal not only to the religious, but very strongly to the ethical and moral tendencies of humanity.

The Remonstrants (formerly Arminians) came upon the scene towards the end of the sixteenth century. Dirk Vorlkertsz Coornhert had written a very able refutation of the dogma of predestination. The Town Council of Amsterdam ordered

Jacob Arminius to write a book against Coornhert's work. But behold! when Arminius settled down to the task, and read Coornhert's argument carefully, he came to the conclusion that the other was right, and from an opponent he turned into a powerful ally. This happy lack of bias has ever been the particular feature of Arminian doctrine, and, like the Mennonites, the Remonstrants hold that the value of religion is determined by its beneficial influence on ethics. Considering the ethical or social fermentation which Holland, like every other country, has witnessed during the last decades, it is not surprising to find a great many "Modern" members of the Netherlands *Hervormde Kerk*, joining the Remonstrant fraternity, which affords absolute liberty as regards dogma and confession, and at the same time satisfies their altruistic inclinations.

It is one of the commonest contentions of the age that ethics and religion can exist in one being independently of each other. One very advanced sect of "Modern Dutch Protestants—not yet, however, numbering a great many adherents—does not go quite to this extreme, but in the *Vrye Gemeente*, or "Free Community," they represent religion as a thing complete in itself, a thing purely pertaining to the individual, personal spiritual life. This "Free Community" was established in 1878 by two Amsterdam ministers, Pieter Hermannus Hugenholtz and Frederik

Religious Life and Thought

Willem Nicolaas Hugenholtz. They neither observe Ascension Day nor Whitsuntide; they have abolished Baptism and the Eucharist; and, however charitable the members may be in their private capacities, the "Free Community," as such, does not practise poor-relief or charity in any form.

In this connexion it is interesting to add a few words about Dutch Free Masonry. The Dutch Free Masons of the present day are not so much moralists as ethicists. The well-being of the commonwealth based upon the well-being of every member—spiritually, intellectually, and materially — is their threefold aim. They feel and express profound admiration for every form of religious life, utterly indifferent as to the existence or non-existence of any dogma accompanying it, since they freely realise how strong a motive religion is to ethics; they admit Roman Catholics, Orthodox or Modern Protestants, Jews, Buddhists, Mohammedans, Atheists, and Agnostics into their fraternity, no confessional test whatever being put to anyone; they only require faithful co-operation towards the general betterment of human society as a whole.

The Hebrew Church has also enjoyed perfect freedom ever since the Constitution of 1848 made the right of congregation absolute and incontestable. But after being fettered during so many centuries, it took even this energetic and tenacious race some twenty years to shake itself free from the lingering influences of long-protracted restraint. It was only in 1870 that the Netherlands Israelitic Congregation was established; the Portuguese Jews in Holland have a separate governing body. Modern and ancient views clash here, as everywhere else, but the consciousness of their illustrious history, not sullied, but adorned with greater brilliancy by centuries of persecution, becomes gradually more powerful in the mind of the Dutch Jew, and invigorates his natural and national tendency towards the ancient rites and doctrines of his classic creed.

CHAPTER XX

THE ARMY AND NAVY

ALTHOUGH the Dutch maintained their independence in the sixteenth century against the most formidable regular army in Europe, and also did their fair share of fighting in the seventeenth and eighteenth centuries, they have long ceased to aspire to the rank of a military Power. The separation from Belgium in 1830–31 put an end to the Orange policy of creating a powerful Netherland State from Lorraine to the North Sea which could hold its own with either France or Prussia, and since that period Holland has gradually sunk, and seemingly without discontent, into the position of a third-rate Power. This has taken place without any apparent loss of the old love of independence, but it has necessarily been accompanied by a diminution not only of the military spirit, but of military efficiency and readiness. The spectacle of immense armies of millions of men in the neighbouring States seems to have produced a sense of helplessness among the people of the Netherlands, and to have led them to believe that resistance, were it needful, would be futile. The inglorious campaign of 1794, when Pichegru occupied Holland almost without a blow, serves as a sort of object-lesson to demonstrate the hopelessness of any attempt at resistance, instead of the creditable campaign of 1793, when the Dutch expelled Dumouriez from their country. Curiously enough, the Transvaal War has revived national hope and confidence by showing what a well-armed people without military training can do when standing on the defensive. Time is necessary to prove whether this new sentiment will remove the fatalistic feeling of helplessness that has been creeping over Dutch public men, and brace them to efforts worthy of their ancestry.

The sense of impotency has not been confined to the land forces alone. In that matter it was felt that a nation of less than five millions could not compete with those that numbered forty and fifty millions. But the same sentiment exists also with regard to maritime power, where the competition is not of men, but of money. The immense navies of modern days, and the enormous cost of their maintenance and renovation, seem to exclude small States from the rank of naval Powers. Holland, with the finest material for manning a navy of any Continental State, can be no exception to the general rule. Her little navy is a model of efficiency, her small cruisers of 5000 tons are not surpassed by any of the same size, and the *morale* of her officers, one may not doubt,

The Army and Navy

is worthy of the service that produced not only the Ruyters and Tromps of old days, but Suffren, our most able opponent during the long Napoleonic struggle. None the less, the Dutch navy remains a small navy, quite overshadowed by the immense organisations of the present age, and without any possible chance of competing with them.

This self-evident fact exercises a depressing influence on Dutch opinion, which has latterly shown a marked desire to ally the country with some other. An alliance with Belgium, that of the North and South Netherlanders, the old Union of the Provinces broken in 1579 and imperfectly restored from 1815 to 1830, would be hailed with delight. The difficulty of attaining this consolidation of Netherland opinion and resources, on account of pronounced religious differences, has resulted in the formation of a considerable body of opinion favourable to an alliance with Germany. For the moment, events in South Africa have placed the old English party in a hopeless minority.

Although the Dutch possess in probably an unabated degree all the sturdy characteristics that distinguished them of old, it seems as if prosperity had somewhat blunted the edge of patriotism, at least to the extent of rendering them unwilling to submit to the hardships of the conscription, when fully applied to the whole people. As a consequence the Dutch do not come under the head of an armed nation, and the war effective of their army is less than 70,000 men.

The regulations applying to the army are based on the law of 1861, which was modified in one important particular by an Act of 1898. The army was to be raised partly by conscription and partly by voluntary enlistment. The annual contingent by conscription was fixed at 11,000 men. Every man became liable to conscription at the age of nineteen, but as the right of purchasing exemption continued in force until the Act of 1898 referred to, all well-to-do persons so minded escaped from the obligation of military service. At the same time its conditions were made as light as possible. Nominally the conscripts had to serve for five years, but in reality they remained one year with the colours, and afterwards were called out for only six weeks' training during each of the four subsequent years. The regular army thus obtained mustered on a peace footing 26,000 men and 2000 officers, and on a war footing 68,000 officers and men and 108 guns, excluding fortress artillery. Considering the interests entrusted to its charge, the Dutch army must be pronounced the weakest of any State possessing colonies — a position of no inconsiderable importance from the historical and political point of view.

It will be said, no doubt, that Holland possesses other land forces besides her regular army, and this is true, but they are by the admission of the

The Army and Navy

Dutch themselves, ill organised and not up to the level of their duties. There is the *Schutterij*, or National Volunteer force—perhaps Militia would be a more correct term, because the law creating it is based on compulsion. The law organising the Schutterij was passed in April, 1827, by which all males were required to serve in it between the ages of twenty-five and thirty, and from thirty to thirty-five in the Schutterij reserve. An active division is formed out of unmarried men and widowers without children. This division would be mobilised immediately on the outbreak of war, and would take its place alongside the regular army. It probably numbers five thousand men out of the total of 45,000 active Schutterij. The reserve Schutterij does not exceed 40,000, but behind all these is what is termed indifferently the *Landsturm* or the *levée en masse*. There is only one defect in this arrangement, which is that by far the larger portion of the population has never had any military training except that given to the Schutterij, which is practically none at all. A *levée en masse* in Holland would have precisely the value, and no more, that it would have in any other non-military State which either did not possess a regular army of adequate efficiency and strength, or which had not passed its population through the ranks of a conscript army.

The Dutch Schutterij is ostensibly based on the model of the Swiss Rifle Clubs, and the obligatory part of its service relates to rifle-practice at the targets, but there the similarity ends. There is no room to question the efficiency of the Swiss marksmen, and the tests applied are very severe. But in Holland the practice is very different. The Schutterij meetings are made the excuse for jollity, eating, and drinking. They are rather picnics than assemblies for the serious purpose of qualifying as national defenders. Even in marksmanship the ranges are so short, and the efficiency expected so meagre, that the military value of this civic force is exceedingly dubious. It could only be compared with that of the Garde Civique of Belgium, and with neither the Swiss Rifle Corps nor our own Volunteers.

Curiously enough, there is, however, an offshoot of the Schutterij based also on the old organisation of an ancient guild called the "Sharpshooters." Its members are supposed to be good shots, or at least to take pains to become so, and they practise at something approaching long ranges. But it is a very limited and somewhat exclusive organisation based on a considerable subscription. It is the society or club of well-to-do persons with a bent towards rifle-practice. An application to the Schutterij of the obligations forming part of the voluntary and self-imposed conditions accepted by the "Sharpshooters" would, no doubt, add much to its efficiency, and might in time give Holland a serviceable auxiliary corps of riflemen.

Besides the home army, Holland possesses a

very considerable Colonial army which is commonly known as the Indian contingent. This force garrisons Java, Sumatra, and the other colonies in the East. The army of the East Indies numbers 13,000 Europeans and 17,000 natives, principally Malays of Java. Besides this regular garrison a Schutterij force is maintained in Java. It consists of 4000 Europeans and 6000 natives. The Europeans are the planters and the members of the civil service. The natives are the retainers of some of the native princes, and the overseers and more responsible men employed on the European plantations. The total garrison of the Dutch East Indies is consequently a very considerable one, viewed by the light of its duties, but allowance has to be made for the interminable war in Atchin, which keeps several thousand men permanently engaged, and never seems nearer an ending.

The Dutch authorities find great difficulty in recruiting their army for the East Indies, and with the growth of prosperity this difficulty increases. Indeed, the garrison could not be maintained at its present high strength but for the numerous volunteers who come forward for this well-paid service from Germany and Belgium. At one time these outside recruits became so numerous owing to the tempting offers made to them by the Dutch authorities that the two Governments interested presented formal protests against their proceedings. Germany has always been very sore on the subject of losing any of her soldiers, and Belgium has much need of all the men likely to serve abroad in the Congo State. There are still foreigners of the German and Belgian races in the Dutch Indian army, but any design of turning it into a Foreign Legion on the same model as that of the force which has served France so well in Algeria and her colonies has fallen through.

The only active service or practical experience of war which the Dutch army has had since the end of the struggle with Belgium has been in the East Indies. The Lombock expedition of 1894 is still remembered for its losses and disasters, but on that occasion the Dutch displayed a fine spirit of fortitude under a reverse, and ended the campaign by bringing the hostile Sultan to reason. The long struggle with the Atchinese has been marked by heroism on both sides, and is evidence that the Dutch have not lost their old tenacity. At the same time the Government finds considerable difficulty in obtaining the requisite number of voluntary exiles to preserve its possessions in the Eastern Archipelago, and it may find itself obliged to reduce the effective strength of its garrison.

Moreover, the hygienic conditions are still extremely unfavourable, and the rate of mortality among Europeans in Java and the Celebes is particularly high. It may be no longer true, as was said with perhaps some exaggeration in the time of Marshal Daendels at the beginning of last century, that the European Dutch garrisons die out every three years, but the death-rate is certainly high and a considerable part of the garrison returns invalided by fever a very few months after its arrival in the East. At present the Dutch Indies are absolutely safe because England does not covet them, and would never dream of molesting the Dutch in them provided she herself remains unmolested. But should international competitions break out in that quarter of the world Holland might experience some difficulty in maintaining her garrison at an adequate strength for the proper discharge of her international duties, but this contingency is not likely to present itself for another twenty or thirty years.

The troops of the regular Dutch army will compare favourably with any of their neighbours. They are not as stiff on parade as the Germans, and they are more solid than the French. Their physique is good, although, owing to the practice of purchasing a substitute, which has too lately ceased to allow of the change to come into full effect, the infantry contains an abnormal number of short men, which gives a misleading idea of the average height of the race. The minimum height of the infantry soldier is 5 ft. 1½ ins., which is very low for a people whose general stature is equal to that of the British. There is certainly one point in which the Dutch soldiers strike the observer as being different from their neighbours. They seem light-hearted and jovial, not at all oppressed by the severe claims of discipline, and at the same time quite free from the slouch that gives the Belgian linesman a non-military appearance.

The strength of the Dutch army lies undoubtedly in its corps of officers, a body of specially qualified men fitted to discharge the duties that devolve on the leaders of any army. The majority of these pass through the Royal Military Academy, an institution from which England might borrow some features with advantage. Candidates are admitted between the ages of fifteen and eighteen, and undergo a course of four years before they are eligible for a commission. As the charges at the Academy are limited to £22 10s. a year, the expense of becoming an officer forms no prohibitive barrier, and in a course of training spread over four years the cadet can be turned into a fully qualified officer before he is entrusted with the discharge of practical duties. Moreover, his training does not stop with his leaving the Academy. It is supposed to be necessary to complete it by a further course in camps of instruction, and subsequently by what are called State missions in the temporary service of other armies. This practice is fairly general on the Continent, although it is never resorted to by the British, who are less acquainted with the organisation of Continental armies than is the case with even third or fourth-rate States.

The headquarters of the Dutch Engineers are at Utrecht, of the Artillery at Zwolle, of the Infantry at The Hague, and of the Cavalry at Breda. Utrecht is the most important of these military stations, because the Engineers are the most important branch of the army, and also because it is the centre of the canal and dyke system of Holland. The school or college of the State Civil Engineers, to whom is entrusted the care of the dykes, is at Utrecht. They are known as *Waterstaat*, and Utrecht may be held to supplement and complete the machinery existing at the capital, Amsterdam, for flooding the country. In theory and on paper, the defence of Holland is based on the assumption that in the event of invasion the country surrounding Amsterdam to as far as Utrecht on one side and Leyden on the other would be flooded. There are many who doubt whether the resolution to sanction the enormous attendant damage would be displayed. It is said that the national spirit does not beat so high as when the youthful William resorted to that measure in 1672 to baffle the French monarch, and then prepared his fleet, in the event of its failure, to convey the relics of Dutch greatness and the fortunes of Orange to a new home and country beyond the seas. On that occasion the waters did their work thoroughly well. But it is said that they might not accomplish what was expected of them on the next occasion, while the damage inflicted would remain. Nothing can solve this question save the practical test, but there is no reason to believe that at heart the Dutch race of to-day is less patriotic or resolute than formerly.

At the same time a very important change has to be noted in the views of Dutch strategists. Formerly the whole system of national defence centred in Amsterdam, and it must be added that the dykes have been mainly constructed with the idea of flooding the country round it. This was the old plan, sanctioned by antiquity and custom, of defending the capital at all costs, and making it the final refuge of the race. But latterly the opinion has been spreading among military men that Rotterdam would make a far better place of final stand than Amsterdam, because the forts of the Texel once forced, the capital might be menaced by a naval attack from the Zuyder Zee or by the Northern Canal. In old days Amsterdam was safe from any naval descent, but the introduction of steam has laid it open to the attack at least of torpedo flotillas. The entrance to the Meuse, it is represented, could be made impregnable with little difficulty, and the approaches to Rotterdam from the land side are far more dependent on the proper restraining of the waters within their artificial or natural channels than those to Amsterdam. There is another argument in support of Rotterdam. It would be easier for Holland's allies to send aid there than to Amsterdam, while a strong position at Rotterdam would seriously menace any hostile army at Utrecht, and contribute materially to the defence of Amsterdam as well. But the Dutch are a slow people to move. Amsterdam is supposed to be ready to stand a siege at any time, whereas Rotterdam's defences are mainly on paper. The garrison of Rotterdam is only a few hundred men, and to convert it into a fortified position would, no doubt, entail the outlay of a good many million florins. Still, the conviction is spreading that Rotterdam has supplanted Amsterdam as the real centre of Dutch prosperity and national life.

The Schutterij is, singularly enough, not popular. The reason for this is not very clear, as the duties are quite nominal, and in no material degree interfere with civil employment. The distaste to any form of military service is tolerably general, and the advanced Radical party has adopted as one of its cries, " Nobody wishes to be a soldier." Probability points, however, not to the abolition of the Schutterij, but to its being made more efficient, and consequently the conditions of service in it must become more rigorous. There is one portion of the duties of the Schutterij which is far from unpopular with the men of the force. When a householder neglects to pay his taxes one or more militiamen are quartered on him, and he is obliged to supply his guests not merely with good food and lodging, but also with abundant supplies of tobacco and gin. Apart from such incidents, which one may not doubt from the nature of the penalty are exceedingly rare, the Schutterij seems to have rather a dull and monotonous time of it.

There is one fact about the Dutch army that deserves mention. It is extremely well behaved, and the men give their officers very little trouble. The discipline is lighter than in most armies. There is an unusually kindly feeling between officers and men for a Continental force, and at the same time the public and the military are on excellent terms with each other. This is, no doubt, due to the very short period served with the colours, and to the fact that the last four years, with the exception of six weeks annually in a camp or fortress, are passed in civil life at home.

The Dutch navy, although small in comparison with its past achievements and with its present competitors, is admitted to be well organised, efficient in its condition, and manned by a fine *personnel*. It is generally said, perhaps unjustly, that the pick of the manhood of Holland joins the navy in preference to the army. One fact shows that there is no difficulty in obtaining the required number of recruits to man the fleet, for while the nominal law is that of conscription for the navy as well as for the army, all the necessary contingent is obtained by voluntary enlistment. No doubt the large fishing and boating classes provide excellent material, and a comparatively short spell of service on board a man-of-war offers an agreeable break in their lives. The Dutch being a nautical race by tradition as well as by the daily work of a large portion of them, there is nothing uncongenial in a naval career. No difficulty is experienced in obtaining the services of the seven thousand seamen and two thousand five hundred marine infantry who form the permanent staff of the Dutch navy, and if the country's finances enabled it to build more ships, there would be no serious difficulty in providing the required number of men to furnish their crews.

In 1897 some steps were taken in this direction, and a credit of five millions sterling for a shipbuilding programme was voted. Its operations have not yet been brought to a conclusion, but a torpedo fleet has been created for the defence of the Zuyder Zee, supplementing the defences at Helder and the Texel. Something has also been done in the same direction for the defence of Batavia and the ports of Java. The Dutch navy might be correctly described as a good little one, quite equal to the everyday work required of it, but not of the size or standard to play an ambitious rôle. We should not, however, overlook the fact that its addition to the navy of another Power would be as important an augmentation of strength as was the case when Pichegru added the Dutch fleet to that of France by capturing it with cavalry and horse artillery while ice-bound in the Zuyder Zee. Nor can we always count on a Duncan to end the story as at Camperdown.

The impression left on an observer of the military and naval classes in Holland is that they are not animated by a very strong martial spirit. Clothed in a military costume, they are still essentially men of peace, who would be sorry to commit an act of violence or do an injury to anyone. The officers as a class are devoted to the technical part of their work, and are thoroughly well posted in the science of war. But whether it is due to the long peace, to the spread of prosperity among all classes of the community, or to the lymphatic character of the race, it is not easy to persuade one's self that the Dutch army, taken as a whole, is a formidable instrument of war.

This feeling must be corrected by a study of history, and by recognising that there are no symptoms of deterioration in the sturdy qualities of the Dutch people. Physically and morally the Netherlanders of to-day are the equals of their forefathers, but the conditions of their national life, the fortunate circumstances that have so long made them unacquainted with the terrible ordeals of war, have diverted their thoughts from a bellicose policy, and have confirmed them in their peaceful leanings. How far these tendencies have diminished their fighting-power, and rendered them unequal to accept or bear the sacrifices that would be entailed by any strenuous defence of their country against serious invasion by a Great Power, must remain a matter of opinion. Perhaps their organisation has become somewhat rusty. Reforms are admitted to be necessary. The annual contingent is altogether too small for the needs of the age ; a great and efficient national reserve should be created ; and in good time the army ought to be raised to the numbers that would enable it to man and hold the numerous and excellent forts which have been constructed at all vital points. The Dutch plans of defence are excellent, but to carry them all out a very considerable army would be necessary, and at the present moment Holland possesses only the skeleton of an army.

Leaving the question of numbers and military organisation aside, only praise can be given to the Dutch soldier individually. He is clean, civil, good-tempered, and with a far closer resemblance to Englishmen in what we regard as essentials than any other Continental. The officers are in the truest sense gentlemen, free from swagger, and not overbearing towards their men and their civilian compatriots. They represent a genuine type of manhood, free from artificiality or falsehood. One feels instinctively that they say what they think, and that they will do rather more instead of less than they promise.

CHAPTER XXI

HOLLAND OVER SEA

HOLLAND holds the second place among the successful colonising nations, though Powers like England, France, and Germany surpass her in the actual area of their colonies and protectorates. Besides her East Indian possessions, which form by far the most important part of her colonial empire, she holds Surinam, or Dutch Guiana, and six small islands, including Curaçao, in the West Indies, and her colonial subjects number in all more than thirty-six millions, being as many as the colonial subjects of France and at least seven times the population of the Netherlands in Europe. The East Indian Archipelago belonging to the Netherlands consists of five large islands and a great number of smaller ones. It is not within the scope of a book like this to go into details of geographical division, but a glance at the map will show us that the three groups which make up this dependency are extended over a length of about three thousand miles, and include Java and Sumatra, Borneo, Celebes, New Guinea, the Timor Laut archipelago, and the Moluccas. The northern part of Borneo is a British possession, and the eastern half of New Guinea is divided between England and Germany, while half of the island of Timor is Portuguese; the rest of the archipelago forms the possession known as Netherlands India, or the Dutch East Indies. The most important and the most densely populated of these islands are Java and Sumatra; at the last census, in 1899, Java alone had twenty-six millions of inhabitants, more than four times as many as in 1826, but the richness of its soil is so great that it could support a much larger population, though the island is only about the same size as England.

Java was taken by the English in 1811 from the French flag, but was restored at the Peace of Vienna to the Netherlands, together with some of the other Dutch colonies. As Dr. Bright remarks in his *History of England*, "It has been believed that its value and wealth were not thoroughly known or appreciated by the Ministry at the time." It has now become by far the most important of the Dutch dependencies, and the favourite colony for fortune-hunters.

Considering the great wealth of the Dutch Indies, it is a little surprising that so few young men are tempted to go out there to seek their fortunes. As is usually the case in the tropics, those parts of the coasts which are low and marshy are very unhealthy for Europeans, who cannot stay in such places for any length of time without falling victims to malaria, though the Malays do not seem to be affected by the climate; but higher up, from 500 to 1000 feet above the sea, it is healthy enough, and up the hills, in the larger islands, the climate leaves little to be desired. The temperature generally varies between 70 and 90 degees all the year round, though there is a certain amount of difference between one island and another. North of the equator the rainy monsoon lasts from October to April, and the dry season from April to October, while on the south side these seasons are reversed. On the line, however, the trade-winds and monsoons appear very irregularly, because there are four seasons instead of two — that is to say, two rainy and two dry — and the weather is also subject to frequent changes of a local character, especially in the neighbourhood of mountain-ranges and volcanoes. With the exception of Borneo and the central part of the Celebes all these islands are volcanic. In the principal group, which stretches from Sumatra and Java to the Timor Laut archipelago, there are no less than thirty-three active volcanoes, of which twelve are in Java, besides a number of so-called extinct ones which may at any moment burst into renewed life. Some of the smaller islands are merely sunken volcanoes, such as Gebeh, for instance, and the Banda Islands, where the "Goonong Api" (Fire-mountain) is a living proof. The best known of all these volcanoes is the terrible

Cracatoa, one of the three which may be seen in the Straits of Sunda. Readers may remember the great eruption of 1886, when half the island of Cracatoa and part of the mountain, which was split clean in two, were swallowed up in the sea, and parts of the coasts of Java and Sumatra were overwhelmed by the tidal wave that accompanied the outburst, ships being lifted bodily on to the land and left perched among the hills. In one day and night 100,000 persons perished, and except a slight earthquake, which, as earthquakes are not uncommon in that part of the world, was naturally not regarded as serious, there was no warning of the impending disaster, for the crater had shown no signs of life for 200 years. During the eruption a roar as of distant artillery could be heard in the middle of Java, fully 400 miles from the scene.

The form of the islands prevents the existence of very large rivers; the largest are in Borneo, the only non-volcanic island in the archipelago which can boast of three navigable rivers each about 400 miles long. Owing to the narrowness of Java and Sumatra, the rivers flowing towards the north-east coasts of these islands are very rapid, and as they are liable to be suddenly swollen by heavy rains, canals have been dug, and others are in course of construction, to ensure a regular outflow and protect the land from floods. In an undertaking of this kind the Dutch are quite at home, for, as everyone knows, they are past-masters in the art of taming the waters; but they have not to push back the sea here, as they have done and are still doing in their native country; the rivers do that for them, by bringing down masses of gravel and mud, which form wide banks at their mouths and are soon overgrown with trees. The light-house at Batavia, in Java, was built about the middle of the seventeenth century at what was then the entrance to the harbour ; now it is two and a half miles from the entrance, the shore having advanced that distance in 250 years.

Before passing to the question of government, it may be well to notice the principal races with which the Dutch have to deal. Besides the native population, the Dutch Indies contained in 1892 about 446,000 Chinese, 20,000 Arabs, and 26,000 other Asiatics, but only 55,000 Europeans, including the soldiers, many of whom are Germans. The greater part of all these are found in Java. Of the remaining 35½ millions the majority are Malays, including Malays proper and several kindred races, and to this last class belong the Javanese, who live in Java, Madura, Bally (or Bali), and Lombok. Natives other than Malays are the Dyaks, in the interior of Borneo, the Battaks, in the interior of Sumatra, and finally the Papuans, who inhabit New Guinea, or Papua, and some of the small islands near. These Papuans are said to be of the same race as the Australian aborigines, and are the only black people in these islands, the other inhabitants being light-brown or copper-coloured. In religion, most of the Malays are Mohammedans, but the people of Bally and Lombok are still Brahmins, while the Dyaks and Battaks are of very primitive faiths. From remote times until 1478 Brahminism and Buddhism were the principal religions, but in that year the faith of Islam began to supersede them. The ancient religions were responsible for a degree of civilisation never arrived at by the Mohammedans, traces of which are seen in the numerous ruins of cities and temples that must have been of great beauty and grandeur which are found in Java, and also in the Javanese literature, which is written in its own peculiar characters, and the *wayangs*, or shadow-plays, which are performed on every festive occasion, and all of which refer to a history of conquest and wars waged in the times of Brahminism.

Here the problem which confronts the Dutch authorities is the old one of uniting under one government populations differing in blood and religion, a problem which always presents great difficulties and even a certain amount of danger. The system adopted resembles, to some extent, that applied to certain native States in British India, and the islands are governed by native kings and princes, under the paternal supervision of the Netherlands India Government, which consists of a Governor-General, or Viceroy, and a Council of four Councillors of State, of which the Viceroy is President. Under these there are three Governors and thirty-four Residents, all Europeans, with several Assistant-Residents and *Controleurs*, each of whom has a district assigned to him, in which he has to maintain order and see that the land is kept in proper cultivation. The Indian princes are made Government officials by the fact of being paid by the Dutch Government, and bear the official titles of Regent, *Demang*, etc., but they also keep their own grander-sounding titles, such as *Raden Adipatti*, and so on, of which they are naturally very proud. It is the duty of a Resident to advise the Regent of his district and at the same time to keep a watch on him and see that he does not oppress his subjects. If a Regent is proved to be guilty of oppression, or in case of sedition or the fostering of rebellion, he is deposed by the Government, and a better man is appointed in his place, if possible one of his own relatives, so that the lower classes may be protected and the authority of the native nobility be upheld at the same time. In some "up-country" districts, in Borneo and Celebes, however, the native rulers are practically independent, and the Dutch Government is not at present inclined to assert its authority by force of arms; while in the northwest of Sumatra, though the Atchinese pirates have at last been suppressed, the war party is not yet extinct.

Throughout these dependencies the aim of the

Government is to rule the inhabitants through men of their own race, not to substitute foreigners for natives ; and if fault can be found with this policy it is that too little restraint is put upon the intermixture of the white and coloured races.

The splendid fertility of the soil and the great quantity of land yet uncultivated naturally led the Dutch to seek some means by which the natural advantages of their islands might be put to better use, and to this end they set to work to overcome the indolent habits of the natives, who were not inclined to do more than they considered necessary for their own subsistence, and to induce them to devote more of their time and energies to agriculture. In return for good roads and bridges and the protection afforded by the Government, the natives were induced to give a certain amount of their time to the cultivation of coffee, sugar, indigo, and other crops. In this way they were taxed not in coin but in labour; and this system, known as the " Culture system," has produced very good results, especially in Java and Madura. Gradually, however, under the influence of the younger members of the governing nation, the cultivation of sugar and partly that of coffee also was dropped by the Government, and left to private enterprise, but, supervision by the Government being thereby abandoned, cases occurred of abuse of power by the *concessionnaires ;* and though much has been done to prevent such abuse, it must be admitted that the condition of native workmen is not so good in the private concessions as it was under the direct authority of the Government.

Meanwhile, the outlook is promising; the development of the natural resources of the islands goes steadily on, though the rate of progress may not be particularly rapid, and the inhabitants are generally peaceful and well-behaved, while their number increases at a rate which seems to indicate continued and growing prosperity. The schools, too, are doing good work, and more and more of the natives are learning the language of their rulers. When a Malay has learned enough Dutch to express himself fairly clearly in that language, he is very proud of the accomplishment, and seldom misses an opportunity of displaying his knowledge.

One of the greatest drawbacks to the moral advance of the native is the bad example set by Europeans, on which it will be needful to say more later. Things are not nearly so bad in this respect as they formerly were, but still the unprincipled life which many of the white men are leading gives rise to doubt in the native mind as to the blessings of Western civilisation.

That the native races are generally well-disposed towards the Dutch is borne out by the number that take service under the Government as police and as soldiers. Every two or three miles along the Government roads in Java one may meet a *Gardoe*, or patrol of the country police, consisting of three bare-footed Javanese constables, in uniform of a semi-European cut and armed with kreeses.

As we have already seen, the army which the Dutch maintain in their East Indian colonies is quite distinct from the home army of Holland. On their arrival the men are quartered in barracks, and the officers and married non-commissioned officers find houses at a moderate rent close by. The barracks consist not of single buildings but of many separate ones, so that the different races among the native troops may be kept distinct. Malays, Javanese, Madurese, Amboinese, Bugis, Macassarese, and the rest must all have separate buildings to themselves. Formerly there were Ashantees too, but the recruiting of these was stopped when the colony of St. George del Mina, on the Gold Coast, was transferred to England on the surrender of British claims in the north of Sumatra; very good soldiers they were, but cruel in war, giving no quarter, and very difficult to restrain in the heat of action. The native troops are officered by Europeans, but the sergeants and corporals are always of the same race as the men under them.

Great care is taken to safeguard the health of the troops, not only in the arrangement of barracks and in the selection of positions for garrisons, which are chosen as much on hygienic as on strategic grounds, but also by the establishment of military hospitals. In most large towns, and in smaller places on the coast where forts have been built, there are military hospitals, and to these any European, whether soldier or civilian, who falls ill is immediately taken; in fact, no others exist, except some sanatoria recently founded in the hills. A naval officer who often visited these hospitals, as well as hospital ships in war time, describes them as "models of neatness, cleanliness, order, and usefulness. Life in such a hospital," he declares, "is a luxury, not to be compared with anything of the kind in neighbouring colonies."

For many years a considerable force has been constantly employed in Atchin, and a number of ships of war have been cruising along the coast to assist in the suppression of piracy.

The Colonial fleet is made up of some warships built in Holland and others built in India, expressly for the Indian service, including a number of small coasting-steamers and sailing-vessels and a steamer or two specially detailed for hydrographical work. The necessity for these last arises from the shoals and coral reefs which abound in the Java and Flores Seas, in the Straits of Macassar, and among the Moluccas, and from the fact that the creeks and river-mouths are very shallow, and full of convenient hiding-places for pirate proas; it is most important, therefore, that both men-of-war and merchantmen should be kept supplied with good charts.

Piracy is an evil which the Colonial fleet is

specially designed to check, and it used to be very bad at one time, before the Ballinese War of 1845. In the year before this, a Dutch merchantman, the *Overyssel*, stranded on the coast of Bally, and the crew were massacred, and ship and cargo looted by the Ballinese. This led to three expeditions; one in 1845, another, which was undertaken with an insufficient force and ended in disaster to the Dutch in 1847, and the third and final one, successfully carried out by an army of 10,000 men and six warships, together with 6000 auxiliary troops from the island of Lombok. But while piracy was thus put down to the east of Java, the Atchinese pirates grew bolder than ever in the west, and complaints from Malay traders who were Netherlands subjects became more and more frequent. Numerous punitive expeditions were sent against the piratical Rajas in the north-west of Sumatra, but in most cases the real culprits escaped. At last, about 1873, the Government resolved to put an end to this state of things, and a force under General van Swieten seized the *Kraton*, or chief fortress. General van der Heyden took over the command in 1877, and soon captured and fortified Kota Raja, and two years later, though his troops suffered heavily from the climate, he had the whole country of Atchin subdued. The Home Government, however, misled by the apparent submission of the enemy, did away with military rule before they had made certain that no treachery was meditated, and on the arrival of a civil Governor all the advantages which had been won were again lost, and at last a state of war had to be proclaimed once more. From that time onward the Atchinese War became a chronic disease, but since an aggressive policy was adopted in 1898 the war party in Atchin has rapidly diminished, and it is now almost extinct. Fighting of a guerrilla kind is reported from time to time, but peace is so far restored that the General is able to send some of his men home, and the people can cultivate their rice-fields and pepper-gardens unmolested. They are for the most part well-disposed towards the Dutch, whose officers, in their proclamations, have always been careful to explain that the war was only against the murderers and robbers who made the coasts and country unsafe, and that no one would be harmed so long as he went peacefully about his business. Piracy on the Atchinese coast is now also a thing of the past, and will be so as long as the Government remains firm.

To turn to more peaceful subjects, Netherlands India is favoured above most lands in the richness and variety of its products, its mineral wealth alone being sufficient to make it a most valuable possession from a commercial point of view. A part of the Government revenue is derived from the sale of tin, which is found in several islands, and coal-fields exist in Sumatra and Laut, while gold is found on the west coast of Borneo and also in Sumatra, where the Ophir district no doubt owes its name to the presence of the precious metal. Another mineral product is petroleum, which has made the fortunes of several lucky colonists; it is found in many places, but the principal supply comes from Sumatra. These are some of the chief products, but they by no means exhaust the list, nor is the wealth of the colonies confined to minerals; there are the pearl-fisheries, for example, amongst the little islands lying south-west of New Guinea, and the Moluccas contribute mother-of-pearl and tortoise-shell, but the real wealth of the islands lies in the extraordinary fertility of the soil. Most of the land is clay, coloured red by the iron ore which it contains, and will grow almost anything, besides being very suitable for making bricks. Sugar, tea, coffee, indigo, and tobacco are grown in large quantities for export, and the principal crops cultivated by the natives are rice (in the marshy districts), maize, cotton, and many kinds of fruit which are also grown in British India. Most of the inhabitants are tillers of the soil, but the maritime natives are naturally occupied chiefly in the fisheries, and it is a very pretty sight, at any little fishing village, to see the boats start out for the hoped-for haul. Just before sunrise scores of little fishing-boats with bamboo masts and huge triangular mat-sails slip out of the creeks before the fresh land-wind, which lasts just long enough to carry them to the fishing-ground in the offing, and about four o'clock in the afternoon a sea-breeze springs up, and back they all come, generally laden with splendid fish. The evening breeze often attains such strength that the little boats would capsize if it were not for a balancing-board pushed out to windward, on which one or two, or sometimes three, men stand to act as a counterpoise, so that it may not be necessary to shorten sail. The Malays excel in boat-building, and rank very high in the art of shaping vessels which offer the least possible resistance to the water, and their boats fly over the surface of the sea in the most wonderful manner. If we except the rude tree-trunks used here and there, the vessels made by the Malays may serve, and have served, as models for swift sailing-craft all over the world.

Amongst the other industries for which the Malays, and the Javanese especially, are noted, the principal is the manufacture of textile fabrics; sometimes these are very skilfully dyed in ornamental patterns, and show considerable artistic taste.

Besides boat-building and weaving, the crafts of the blacksmith and carpenter should be mentioned, and also that of the gold and silversmith, for this indicates the source of many of the treasures with which wealthy Dutch homes in the old country abound.

Now that the war in Atchin is practically over it is not unlikely that the next few years may see greater advances in the commerce and industries

Holland over Sea

of Netherlands India, especially as the trade returns report that a great industrial awakening is taking place at the present time in Holland, in which case there will be a rush of emigrants to the colonies. As has been said before, the climate out there is not unhealthy as a rule, but of course Europeans have to adapt their life to their surroundings. Profiting by the example of the natives, they have learned to make their houses very airy and cool. A large overhanging roof shades the entrances, front and rear, and the windows are without glass, except in the old cities, its place being taken by bamboo Venetian blinds. Verandahs run along the front and back of the house, which has generally one story only, and never more than two, and the rooms open either on these verandahs or on a central room which divides the house through the middle. The kitchen and store-rooms are in outbuildings at the back, and the garden all round the house is planted with cocoanut, banana, and mango trees, for the sake of their shade as well as for the fruit.

On paying a visit to such a house you go up two or three steps on to the front verandah, where a servant-boy offers you a chair and a drink, and then goes to find his master, who presently joins you. You are never asked to "come in"; if the front verandah is too hot, an adjournment is made to the back. Sometimes, in the interior of the country, visitors are received in the garden, where they enjoy their cheroot Indian fashion, reclining rather than sitting. But this *dolce far niente* does not kill work, for merchants in the towns work pretty hard, and have to be at their offices during the heat of the day, from nine to five, and even on Sunday, if it happens to be mail-day. Other people take life rather easier, especially in the country, where the routine is as follows, more or less : rise at six, bathe, breakfast at seven ; then dress and go to work at nine ; at twelve o'clock lunch, after which one lies down to sleep or read for a couple of hours ; tea at four, and then a second bath. After five it is cool enough to dress and go for a walk or drive until dinner-time, and after dinner you may go for another drive or visit your neighbours. On Sundays you go to church from eleven to twelve, and take things easy for the rest of the day.

Travelling, if for any distance, is done at night, both by Europeans and natives, and if a native has to walk far he usually carries a mat, and when the day begins to get hot he unrolls his mat and lies down on it by the roadside. It does not surprise anyone, therefore, to find seeming idlers asleep in the daytime along the roadside. Naturally, the little wayside shops which are found at every corner are not shut up or removed at night, as most of their trade is done then, but if customers are few the shopkeeper will fall asleep among his wares. The Government roads are well guarded by the native police, and at regular intervals there are stations where fresh horses can be procured, if they are bespoken in time by letter or telegraph.

The colonist's life does not seem to be a very hard one on the whole, though no doubt there are drawbacks, such as, for instance, the want of schools. At present many Dutch children born in India are sent to Holland to be educated, not, as in the case of Anglo-Indians, for the sake of their health, but because there is not a sufficient number of schools in these colonies. This want will be remedied in time, so that colonists may be spared the trouble and expense of sending their children to Europe; but the only Dutch schools in Java that I know of are the *Gymnasium* at Willem III. (Batavia) and one high school for girls. Native schools are more numerous, and are being multiplied not only by the Government but by the missionaries. The attitude of the Indian Government towards missionary work has changed immensely for the better in the last forty years, and the labours of the missionaries are now appreciated very highly by both the Indian and the Home Government, and deservedly so, for the task of the Government has been very much lightened through the improvement in the attitude of the natives, owing largely to the work of the missions.

As to the life and customs of the natives, it is not necessary to describe all the different races,

but the Malay villages deserve notice. In Java
and Sumatra these are not arranged in streets,
but the houses are grouped under large trees, and
are separated from the road by a bamboo fence,
on the top of which notice-boards are fixed at intervals bearing the names of the villages ; these
are necessary, because it is often difficult to see
where one village ends and the next begins. In
the open spaces may be seen a few sacred *warin-
gin* trees, in which are hung wooden bells, used
to sound an alarm or call the villagers together.
Before the house of a native Regent is an open
square, with a *pandoppo*, or roof on pillars, in
the centre, and here meetings are held, proclamations read, and distinguished visitors received.
The houses are built of bamboo and roofed with
palm-leaves; and sometimes they have floors of
split bamboo, but often the hard clay soil serves
as a floor. There are usually two or more sleep-
ing-places, called *balé-balés*, also made of bamboo, split and plaited, and over these another
floor, which forms a sort of loft or store-room.
There is no fireplace, all the cooking being done
outside. Such a house can be bought for about
five shillings ! It takes a few men two or three
weeks to build one, but to take it down and remove it to a new site is a matter of only a few
hours. Near the houses are the stables, where
the buffaloes and carts are kept, and here and
there is a well, over which hangs a balancing-pole,
with a bucket at one end and a stone at the other.

The children play about naked until they are ten years old, when they dress like their elders, and consider themselves men and women. The costume of the Malay women consists of the *sarong* a cloth about 3½ yards long and 1½ wide, which is wound round the body and held by a belt and then rolled up just above the feet; over this a wide coat called a *kabaya* is worn, and over all a *slendang*, which is very much like a *sarong*, but is worn hanging over one shoulder, and in this is slung anything too large to be easily carried in the hands—even the baby. The men wear either *sarongs*, or trousers, or both, and a cotton jacket, and are always armed either with kreeses or chopping-knives, carried in their belts; the weapons are for cutting down cocoanuts and bamboo, and for protection against snakes and tigers. Both sexes wear their hair long, the men with head-cloths and the women with flowers and herbs, and all go barefooted. The men are very good horsemen, and ride, like the Zulus and other coloured men, with only their big toes in the stirrups.

In Bally and Lombok the inhabitants are of the same race as the people of Java and Sumatra, but differ in religion and habits, having never been wholly subjected by the Mohammedans. The difference is chiefly noticeable in the construction of their houses, which are of stone in many cases, and built in streets. Each house has three compartments and a fireplace, or altar, which stands in the middle, opposite the door; the floors are sometimes paved, and the roofs are often covered with tiles instead of leaves, and supported by carved pillars.

These Brahmins have numerous temples, which are quite different from anything in the neighbouring islands, being built of brick and divided into sections by low walls, but without roofs; walls and gates are painted red, white, and blue, and inside stand a number of altars, on which offerings are laid. Brahminism survives in some of the other islands, at some distance from the coast, and occasionally a religious festival ends in a riot between Brahmins and Mohammedans.

The staple food of the Malay races is rice, which is cooked very dry, with fried or dried fish or shrimps and vegetables, and flavoured with chilis, onions, and salt. Dried beef and venison are also used, and wild pig and chickens and ducks are plentiful; other articles of food being maize, sweet potatoes, and many kinds of fruit, such as cocoanuts, bananas, mangoes, mangusteens, and so on. In the Moluccas the staple crop is not rice, but sago, which is prepared from the sap of the sago-palm. To an inhabitant of Java or Sumatra the cocoanut tree is indispensable; when a child is born, a nut is planted, and later on, if the child asks how old he is, his mother shows him the young palm, and tells him that he is " as old as that cocoanut tree." The nuts are boiled for the oil, and the white flesh is eaten, cooked in various ways, generally with other food. All kinds of provisions and other goods, from butcher's meat to needles and thread, are sold at the *passars*, or markets, which are attended by large crowds.

Mention has been made of the moral example set by some Europeans to the natives. Generally the relations between the white and coloured races are those of superiors and inferiors, but in the matter of matrimony there is a difference. Many white men in Netherlands India never dream of marrying; they take to themselves *njais*, or housekeepers. The same thing is done in other colonies, at least in provinces far removed from European society, when native customs allow it. The ancient customs of the Malays and Javanese did not prescribe any religious ceremony for marriages; they had their *adat*, or customs, which were as strictly adhered to as if they had been religious, but there was nothing consecrating the marriage-tie. Moreover, their notions of hospitality, which are similar to those of most primitive races, no doubt encouraged the above-mentioned free marriages, or at least they explain how it was that the Malay women had no objection to becoming the *njais* of Europeans. Where such a woman was the daughter of a prince or chief, the European who took her was invariably some high official, whose position brought him into contact with noble Javanese families. These young women are remarkably graceful, even fascinating, and, besides, have received a good Javanese education, and it is not surprising that such "marriages" were sometimes happy and permanent.

The sons were sent to Europe to be educated, being entrusted to the care of a guardian, uncle, or friend, and on their return to India soon found employment in the service of the Government; the girls stayed at home, and generally married well.

Such instances, however, are rare; more often the man regarded his *njai* merely as a temporary helpmate, and if he saw a chance would marry some rich European girl, when the Indian wife would be set aside—" sent into the bush," as the phrase was. That such behaviour should have roused the wrath and hatred of the discarded wives and their relatives was but natural. Often the European bride, sometimes the faithless husband too, fell by the hand of a murderer who could never be found, or was poisoned by a maid-servant or cook who was bought over to assist in the work of vengeance. The cast-out children sometimes played a part in these tragedies; if not, they certainly retained a hatred of Europeans generally, and rumours of mutiny were the consequence.

How this state of things can be remedied is a question which has long occupied the attention of the Government. Gradually, however, the mixed population is becoming more educated, and can find employment in Government and mercantile offices, as all excel in beautiful handwriting. A better feeling generally exists, and a keener sense of social duty is coming over the Europeans, so that a good many have really married the mothers of their children, a thing which fifty years ago was never heard of. There now exists a mixed race of Eurasians, children of the children of European fathers and Indian mothers, which at one time threatened to become a source of danger and insurrection, but all fear of trouble in that quarter is past. Of the "inland children" many are now receiving a good education. In the Government schools they can learn enough to hold their own in point of knowledge against a large proportion of the Europeans in the colony, and they find employment in offices and shops, on the railway and post-office staffs, and on public works almost as quickly as pure whites.

INDEX

ADMINISTRATIVE system, 76
Amusements, national, 32
Army, the, 247, 273
Art, modern, 180

CANALS and their population, the, **63**
Capital, life in the, 6, 15
Capital punishment, 234
Characteristics, national, 1
Christmas customs, 101
Church, relation of State to, 236
Churches, Dutch, 79, 235
Clergymen, Dutch, 26, 43, 78
Colonies, the Dutch, 253, 264
Costumes, rural, 46, 83, 91
Court, the, 11
Customs, popular, 94, 99, 114, **132**

DIVORCE, the law of, 233
Dykes, the, 63, 257

EASTER customs, 100
Education, public, 30, 72, 154

FARMS and farmers, 76, 83
Freemasonry, Dutch, 245
Friendly Societies, 58
Funerals, customs at, 110

Index

GAMES, children's, 135
Girls, freedom of Dutch, 44

HOME life, 21, 37, 48, 51, 88

INDIES, the Dutch, 264

JUSTICE, administration of, **221**

KERMIS, the, 114

LABOUR, conditions of, 50
Law court, description of a Dutch, **226**
Literature and literary life, 185, 193

MARRIAGE and marriage customs, 47, **103**
Music, 145

NATIONAL characteristics, 1; types, **5**
Navy, the, 248
Newspapers, the, 199

Palm Paaschen, 100
Peasantry, the, 7, 76, 83
Poets, modern Dutch, 188, **190**
Political life and parties, 207
Press, the, 199
Professional classes, the, **21**

QUEEN Wilhelmina, 11

READERS, the Dutch as, **193**
Reading Societies, 196
Religious life, 235
Renaissance, the literary, **187**
Rommelpot, 101
Rural customs, 94, 99, 114

Index

SCHOOLS, the, 30, 72, 154
Sculpture in Holland, 184
Skaters, the Dutch as, 138
Social life, 37
Society, Dutch, 11, 35
Song, national love of, 145
State, relation of Church to, 235
St. Nicholas, festival of, 114, **121**
Student life, 169
Sunday in the country, 79, 133

THEATRE, the, 147
Thrift, Dutch, 7

UNIVERSITIES, the, **167**

VILLAGE life, 76

WAGES of labour, 50, 97
Wedding customs, 47, 103
Women, position of, 37
Working classes, the, 50.

THE END

*A Selection from the
Catalogue of*

G. P. PUTNAM'S SONS

Complete Catalogue sent
on application

Our European Neighbours

Edited by WILLIAM HARBUTT DAWSON

12°. Illustrated. Each, net $1.20
By Mail 1.30

I.—FRENCH LIFE IN TOWN AND COUNTRY
By HANNAH LYNCH.

"Miss Lynch's pages are thoroughly interesting and suggestive. Her style, too, is not common. It is marked by vivacity without any drawback of looseness, and resembles a stream that runs strongly and evenly between walls. It is at once distinguished and useful. . . . Her five-page description (not dramatization) of the grasping Paris landlady is a capital piece of work. . . . Such well-finished portraits are frequent in Miss Lynch's book, which is small, inexpensive, and of a real excellence."—*The London Academy*.

"Miss Lynch's book is particularly notable. It is the first of a series describing the home and social life of various European peoples—a series long needed and sure to receive a warm welcome. Her style is frank, vivacious, entertaining, captivating, just the kind for a book which is not at all statistical, political, or controversial. A special excellence of her book, reminding one of Mr. Whiteing's, lies in her continual contrast of the English and the French, and she thus sums up her praises: 'The English are admirable: the French are lovable.' "—*The Outlook*.

II.—GERMAN LIFE IN TOWN AND COUNTRY
By W. H. DAWSON, author of "Germany and the Germans," etc.

"The book is as full of correct, impartial, well-digested, and well-presented information as an egg is of meat. One can only recommend it heartily and without reserve to all who wish to gain an insight into German life. It worthily presents a great nation, now the greatest and strongest in Europe."—*Commercial Advertiser*.

III.—RUSSIAN LIFE IN TOWN AND COUNTRY
By FRANCIS H. E. PALMER, sometime Secretary to H. H. Prince Droutskop-Loubetsky (Equerry to H. M. the Emperor of Russia).

"We would recommend this above all other works of its character to those seeking a clear general understanding of Russian life, character, and conditions, but who have not the leisure or inclination to read more voluminous tomes. . . . It cannot be too highly recommended, for it conveys practically all that well-informed people should know of 'Our European Neighbours.' "—*Mail and Express*.

IV.—DUTCH LIFE IN TOWN AND COUNTRY

By P. M. HOUGH, B.A.

"There is no other book which gives one so clear a picture of actual life in the Netherlands at the present date. For its accurate presentation of the Dutch situation in art, letters, learning, and politics as well as in the round of common life in town and city, this book deserves the heartiest praise."—*Evening Post.*

"Holland is always interesting, in any line of study. In this work its charm is carefully preserved. The sturdy toil of the people, their quaint characteristics, their conservative retention of old dress and customs, their quiet abstention from taking part in the great affairs of the world are clearly reflected in this faithful mirror. The illustrations are of a high grade of photographic reproductions."—*Washington Post.*

V.—SWISS LIFE IN TOWN AND COUNTRY

By ALFRED T. STORY, author of the "Building of the British Empire," etc.

"We do not know a single compact book on the same subject in which Swiss character in all its variety finds so sympathetic and yet thorough treatment; the reason of this being that the author has enjoyed privileges of unusual intimacy with all classes, which prevented his lumping the people as a whole without distinction of racial and cantonal feeling."—*Nation.*

"There is no phase of the lives of these sturdy republicans, whether social or political, which Mr. Story does not touch upon; and an abundance of illustrations drawn from unhackneyed subjects adds to the value of the book."—*Chicago Dial.*

VI.—SPANISH LIFE IN TOWN AND COUNTRY

By L. HIGGIN.

"Illuminating in all of its chapters. She writes in thorough sympathy, born of long and intimate acquaintance with Spanish people of to-day."—*St. Paul Press.*

"The author knows her subject thoroughly and has written a most admirable volume. She writes with genuine love for the Spaniards, and with a sympathetic knowledge of their character and their method of life."—*Canada Methodist Review.*

VII.—ITALIAN LIFE IN TOWN AND COUNTRY

By LUIGI VILLARI.

"A most interesting and instructive volume, which presents an intimate view of the social habits and manner of thought of the people of which it treats."—*Buffalo Express.*

"A book full of information, comprehensive and accurate. Its numerous attractive illustrations add to its interest and value. We are glad to welcome such an addition to an excellent series."—*Syracuse Herald.*

VIII.—DANISH LIFE IN TOWN AND COUNTRY

By JESSIE H. BROCHNER.

"Miss Brochner has written an interesting book on a fascinating subject, a book which should arouse an interest in Denmark in those who have not been there, and which can make those who know and are attracted by the country very homesick to return."—*Commercial Advertiser.*

"She has sketched with loving art the simple, yet pure and elevated lives of her countrymen, and given the reader an excellent idea of the Danes from every point of view."—*Chicago Tribune.*

IX.—AUSTRO=HUNGARIAN LIFE IN TOWN AND COUNTRY

By FRANCIS H. E. PALMER, author of "Russian Life in Town and Country," etc.

"No volume in this interesting series seems to us so notable or valuable as this on Austro-Hungarian life. Mr. Palmer's long residence in Europe and his intimate association with men of mark, especially in their home life, has given to him a richness of experience evident on every page of the book."—*The Outlook.*

"This book cannot be too warmly recommended to those who have not the leisure or the spirit to read voluminous tomes of this subject, yet we wish a clear general understanding of Austro-Hungarian life."—*Hartford Times.*

X.—TURKISH LIFE IN TOWN AND COUNTRY

By L. M. J. GARNETT.

"The general tone of the book is that of a careful study, the style is flowing, and the matter is presented in a bright, taking way."—*St. Paul Press*.

"To the average mind the Turk is a little better than a bloodthirsty individual with a plurality of wives and a paucity of virtues. To read this book is to be pleasantly disillusioned."—*Public Opinion*.

XI.—BELGIAN LIFE IN TOWN AND COUNTRY

By DEMETRIUS C. BOULGER

"Mr. Boulger has given a plain, straight-forward account of the several phases of Belgian Life, the government, the court, the manufacturing centers and enterprises, the literature and science, the army, education and religion, set forth informingly."—*The Detroit Free Press*.

"The book is one of real value conscientiously written, and well illustrated by good photographs."—*The Outlook*.

XII.—SWEDISH LIFE IN TOWN AND COUNTRY

By G. VON HEIDENSTAM.

"As we read this interesting book we seem to be wandering through this land, visiting its homes and schools and churches, studying its government and farms and industries, and observing the dress and customs and amusements of its healthy and happy people. The book is delightfully written and beautifully illustrated."—*Presbyterian Banner*.

"In this intimate account of the Swedish people is given a more instructive view of their political and social relations than it has been the good fortune of American readers heretofore to obtain."—*Washington Even. Star*.

Our Asiatic Neighbours

12°. Illustrated. Each, net $1.20
By mail 1.30

I.—INDIAN LIFE IN TOWN AND COUNTRY

By Herbert Compton.

"Mr. Compton's book is the best book on India, its life and its people, that has been published in a long time. The reader will find it more descriptive and presenting more facts in a way that appeals to the man of English speech than nine-tenths of the volumes written by travellers. It sets forth the experiences of a quarter of a century, and in that period a man can learn a good deal, even about an alien people and civilization, if he keeps his eyes open. If the other volumes in the series are as good as 'Indian Life in Town and Country' it will score a decided success."—*Brooklyn Eagle.*

"An account of nativelife in India written from the point of view of a practical man of affairs who knows India from long residence. It is bristling with information, brisk and graphic in style, and open-minded and sympathetic in feeling."—*Cleveland Leader.*

II.—JAPANESE LIFE IN TOWN AND COUNTRY

By George William Knox, D.D.

"The childlike simplicity, yet innate complexity of the Japanese temperament, the strangely mingled combination of new and old, important and worthless, poetic and commercial instincts, aims, and ambitions now at work in the land of the cherry blossom are well brought out by Dr. Knox's conscientious representation. The book should be widely read and studied, being eminently reasonable, readable, reliable, and informative."—*Record-Herald.*

"A delightful book, all the more welcome because the ablest scholar in Japanese Confucianism that America has yet produced has here given us impressions of man and nature in the Archipelago."—*Evening Post.*

III.—CHINESE LIFE IN TOWN AND COUNTRY

By E. BARD. Adapted by H. TWITCHELL.

Every phase of Chinese life is touched on, explained, and made clear in this volume. The nation's customs, its traits, its religion, and its history, are all outlined here, and the book should be of great value in arriving at a better understanding of a people and a country about which there has been so much misconception. The illustrations add greatly to the value of the book.

IV.—AUSTRALIAN LIFE IN TOWN AND COUNTRY

By E. C. BULEY.

A bright, readable description of life in a fascinating and little-known country. The style is frank, vivacious, entertaining, captivating, just the kind for a book which is not at all statistical, political, or controversial.

V.—PHILIPPINE LIFE IN TOWN AND COUNTRY

By JAMES A. LEROY.

Mr. LeRoy is eminently fitted to write on life in the Philippines. He was for several years connected with the Department of the Interior in the Philippine Government, when he made a special investigation of conditions in the islands. Since his return he has continued his studies and is already known as an authority on the Philippines. His book gives a full description of life among the native tribes, and also in the Spanish and American communities.